The Constitution of the
State of West Virginia:
Q Quick Reference Guide

Bootblack Budget Books
Copyright 2018 ©
ISBN-13: 978-1726472678
ISBN-10: 1726472671

Contents:

Preamble – Page 22

> **Article I: Relations to the US Government** – Page 23

Section 1. Relations to the Government of the United States

Section 2. Internal Government and Police

Section 3. Continuity of Constitutional Operation

Section 4. Representatives to Congress

Article II: The State – Page 24

Section 1. The State

Section 2. Powers of government in citizens.

Section 3. Requisites of Citizenship.

Section 4. Equal Representation

Section 5. Provisions Regarding Property

Section 6. Treason, What Constitutes/Penalty

Section 7. "Montani Semper Liberi" State Seal

Section 8. Writs, Commissions, Official Bonds/Indictments

Article III: Bill of Rights – Page 26

Section 1. Bill of Rights

Section 2. Magistrates Servants of People

Section 3. Rights Reserved to People

Section 4. Writ of Habeas Corpus

Section 5. Excessive Bail Not Required

Section 6. Unreasonable Searches and Seizures Prohibited

Section 7. Freedom of Speech and Press Guaranteed

Section 8. Relating To Civil Suits for Libel

Section 9. Private Property, How Taken

Section 10. Safeguards For Life, Liberty and Property

Section 11. Political Tests Condemned

Section 12. Military Subordinate To Civil Power

Section 13. Right of Jury Trial

Section 14. Trials of Crimes/Provisions in Interest of Accused

Section 15. Religious Freedom Guaranteed

Section 15a. Voluntary Contemplation, Meditation or Prayer iin Schools

Section 16. Right Of Public Assembly Held Inviolate

Section 17. Courts Open To All/Justice Administered Speedily

Section 18. Conviction not to Work Corruption of Blood or Forfeiture

Section 19. Hereditary Emoluments, Etc., Provided Against

Section 20. Preservation of Free Government

Section 21. Jury Service for Women

Section 22. Right to Keep and Bear Arms

Article IV: Election & Officers – Page 32

Section 1. Election and Officers

Section 2. Mode of Voting by Ballot

Section 4. Persons Entitled to Hold Office/Age Requirements

Section 5. Oath or Affirmation to Support the Constitution

Section 6. Provisions for Removal of Officials

Section 7. General Elections, When Held/Terms of Officials

Section 8. Further Provisions Regarding State's Officers and Agents

Section 9. Impeachment of Officials

Section 10. Fighting of Duels Prohibited

Section 11. Safeguards for Ballots

Section 12. Registration Laws Provided For

Article V: Division of Powers – Page 36

Section 1. Division of Powers

Article VI: The Legislature – Page 37

Section 1. The Legislature

Section 2. Composition of Senate and House of Delegates

Section 3. Senators and Delegates/Terms of Office

Section 4. Division of State into Senatorial Districts

Section 5. Senatorial Districts Designated

Section 6. Provision for Delegate Representation

Section 7. After Census, Delegate Apportionment

Section 8. Designation of delegate districts

Section 9. Further apportionments

Section 10. Arrangement of Senatorial and Delegate Districts

Section 11. Additional Territory may be Admitted into State

Section 12. Senators and Delegates Required to be Residents of Districts

Section 13. Eligibility to Seat in Legislature

Section 14. Bribery Conviction Forfeits Eligibility

Section 15. Senators and Delegates not to Hold Civil Office for Profit

Section 16. Oath of Senators And Delegates

Section 17. Members of Legislature Privileged From Civil Arrest

Section 18. Time and Place of Assembly of Legislature

Section 19. Convening of Legislature by Governor

Section 20. Seat of Government

Section 21. Provisions for Assembling of Legislature Other Than at the Seat of Government

Section 22. Length of Legislative Session

Section 23. Concerning Adjournment

Section 24. Rules Governing Legislative Proceedings

Section 25. Authority to Punish Members

Section 26. Provisions for Undisturbed Transaction of Business

Section 27. Accounting for State Moneys

Section 28. Origination of Bills

Section 29. Requirement for Reading of Bills

Section 30. Acts to Embrace But One Object/Time of Effect

Section 31. How Bills may be Amended

Section 32. "Majority" Defined

Section 33. Compensation and Expenses of Members

Section 34. Distribution of Laws and Journals Provided for, Contracts for Printing

Section 35. State not to be Made Defendant in any Court

Section 36. Lotteries; Bingo; Raffles; County Option

Section 37. Terms of Office not to be Extended After Election

Section 38. Salaries of Officials Cannot be Increased During Official Terms

Section 39. Local Laws not to be Passed in Enumerated Cases

Section 39a. Home Rule for Municipalities

Section 40. Limiting Powers of Court or Judge

Section 41. Each House to Keep Journal of Proceedings

Section 42. Appropriation Bills to be Specific

Section 43. Board Or Court Of Registration Of Voters Prohibited

Section 44. Election of Legislative, County and Municipal Officers

Section 45. Bribery and Attempt to Bribe/Punishment

Section 46. Manufacture and Sale of Liquor

Section 47. Incorporation of Religious Denominations Prohibited

Section 48. Homestead Exemption

Section 49. Property of Married Woman

Section 51. Budget and Supplementary Appropriation Bills

Section 52. Revenues Applicable to Roads

Section 53. Forestry Amendment

Section 54. Continuity of Government amendment

Section 55. Revenues and properties applicable to fish and wildlife conservation

Section 56. Revenues Applicable to Non-game Wildlife Resources in the State

Article VII: Executive Department – Page 64

Section 1. Executive Department

Section 2. Election

Section 3. Certification of Election Returns/Contests

Section 4. Eligibility

Section 5. Chief Executive/Powers

Section 6. Governor's Message

Section 7. Extraordinary Legislative Sessions

Section 8. Governor to Nominate Certain Officers

Section 9. Recess Vacancies/How Filled

Section 10. Governor's Power of Removal

Section 11. Executive May Remit Fines and Forfeitures

Section 12. Governor Commander-In-Chief of Military Forces

Section 13. Official Bond of State Officers

Section 14. Governor's Approval or Disapproval of Bills Passed by the Legislature

Section 15. Governor's Approval or Disapproval of Bills Making Appropriations of Money

Section 16. Vacancy in Governorship, How Filled

Section 17. Vacancies in Other Executive Departments

Section 18. Executive Heads to Make Reports

Section 19. Salaries of Officials

Article VIII: Judicial Power – Page 71

Section 1. Judicial Power

Section 2. Supreme Court of Appeals

Section 3. Supreme Court of Appeals; Jurisdiction and Powers; Officers and Employees; Terms

Section 4. Writ of Error, Supersedeas and Appeal; Scope and Form of Decisions

Section 5. Circuit Courts

Section 6. Circuit Court; Jurisdiction, Authority and Power

Section 7. General Provisions Relating to Justices, Judges, and Magistrates.

Section 8. Censure, Temporary Suspension and Retirement of Justices, Judges and Magistrates; Removal

Section 9. Clerks of Circuit Courts

Section 10. Magistrate Courts

Section 11. Municipal Courts

Section 12. Issuance and Execution of Writs, Warrants and Process; Admission to Bail

Section 13. Parts of Existing Law Effective

Section 14. Pending Causes; Transfer of Causes; Records

Section 15. Offices Phased Out; Effective Date of Article; Certain Provisions to be Operable at Time Specified; Effect of Article on Certain Provisions of Constitution

Section 16. Family Courts

Article IX: County Organization – Page 85

Section 1. County Organization

Section 3. Sheriffs

Section 4. Malfeasance and Misfeasance in Office

Section 5. Commissioning of Officers not Otherwise Provided For

Section 6. Compensation/Deputies

Section 7. Conservators of the Peace

Section 8. Formation of New Counties

Section 9. County Commissions

Section 10. Terms of Office of County Commissioners

Section 11. Powers of County Commissions

Section 12. Clerk of County Commission

Section 13. Reformation of County Commissions

Article X: Taxation And Finance – Page 90

Section 1. Taxation and Finance

Section 1a. Exemptions From and Additional Adjustments to Ad Valorem Property Taxation

Section 1b. Property Tax Limitation and Homestead Exemption Amendment of 1982

Section 1c. Exemption From Ad Valorem Taxation of Certain Personal Property of Inventory and Warehouse Goods, With Phase in to Full Exemption Over Five-Year Period

Section 2. Repealed

Section 3. Receipts and Expenditures of Public Moneys

Section 4. Limitation on Contracting of State Debt

Section 5. Power of Taxation

Section 6. Credit of State not to be Granted in Certain Cases

Section 7. Duties of County Authorities in Assessing Taxes

Section 8. Bonded Indebtedness of Counties, Etc.

Section 9. Municipal Taxes to be Uniform

Section 10. School Levy and Bond Amendment.

Section 11. County and Municipal Excess Levy Amendment

Section 12. Nonprofit Youth Organization Revenue Exemption

Article XI: Corporations – Page 105

Section 1. Corporations

Section 2. Corporate Liability for Indebtedness

Section 3. Exclusive Privileges Prohibited

Section 4. Rights of Stockholders

Section 5. Street Railroads

Section 6. Banks

Section 7. Railroads

Section 8. Rolling Stock Considered Personal Property

Section 9. Railroads Public Highways

Section 10. Stations to be Established

Section 11. Competing Lines/Legislative Permission

Section 12. Right of Eminent Domain

Article XII: Education – Page 109

Section 1. Education

Section 2. Supervision of Free Schools

Section 3. County Superintendents

Section 4. Existing Permanent and Invested School Fund

Section 5. Support of Free Schools

Section 6. School Districts

Section 7. Levies for School Purposes

Section 8. Repealed

Section 9. Certain Acts Prohibited

Section 10. Creation of Independent Free School Districts

Section 11. Appropriation for State Normal Schools

Section 12. Legislature to Foster General School Improvements

Article XIII: Land Titles – Page 113

Section 1. Land Titles

Section 2. Land Entry Prohibited

Section 3. Repealed

Section 4. Repealed

Section 5. Repealed

Section 6. Repealed

Article XIV: Amendments – Page 114

Section 1. Amendments

Section 2. How Amendments are Made

Amendments to the Constitution – Page 116

Amendment 1. THE JUDICIAL AMENDMENT

Amendment 2. THE IRREDUCIBLE SCHOOL FUND AMENDMENT

Amendment 3. THE GOOD ROADS AMENDMENT OF 1920

Amendment 4. THE GOOD ROADS AMENDMENT OF 1928

Amendment 5. FIFTY MILLION DOLLAR BOND ISSUE FOR ROADS AMENDMENT

Amendment 6. VETERANS BONUS AMENDMENT

Amendment 7. KOREAN VETERANS BONUS AMENDMENT

Amendment 8. BETTER ROADS AMENDMENT

Amendment 9. ROADS DEVELOPMENT AMENDMENT

Amendment 10. BETTER SCHOOL BUILDINGS AMENDMENT

Amendment 11. BETTER HIGHWAYS AMENDMENT

Amendment 12. VIETNAM VETERANS BONUS AMENDMENT

Amendment 13. QUALIFIED VETERANS HOUSING BONDS AMENDMENT.

Amendment 14. VETERANS BONUS AMENDMENT

Amendment 15. INFRASTRUCTURE IMPROVEMENT AMENDMENT

Amendment 16. SAFE ROADS AMENDMENT OF 1996

Amendment 17. VETERANS BONUS AMENDMENT

Amendment 18. Roads to Prosperity Amendment of 2017

PREAMBLE

Since through Divine Providence we enjoy the blessings of civil, political and religious liberty, we, the people of West Virginia, in and through the provisions of this Constitution, reaffirm our faith in and constant reliance upon God and seek diligently to promote, preserve and perpetuate good government in the state of West Virginia for the common welfare, freedom and security of ourselves and our posterity.

ARTICLE I: RELATIONS TO THE US GOVERNMENT

Section 1. Relations to the Government of the United States

The state of West Virginia is, and shall remain, one of the United States of America. The constitution of the United States of America, and the laws and treaties made in pursuance thereof, shall be the supreme law of the land.

Section 2. Internal Government and Police

The government of the United States is a government of enumerated powers, and all powers not delegated to it, nor inhibited to the states, are reserved to the states or to the people thereof. Among the powers so reserved to the states is the exclusive regulation of their own internal government and police; and it is the high and solemn duty of the several departments of government, created by this constitution, to guard and protect the people of this state from all encroachments upon the rights so reserved.

Section 3. Continuity of Constitutional Operation

The provisions of the constitution of the United States, and of this state, are operative alike in a period of war as in time of peace, and any departure therefrom, or violation thereof, under the plea of necessity, or any other plea, is subversive of good government, and tends to anarchy and despotism.

Section 4. Representatives to Congress

For the election of representatives to Congress, the state shall be divided into districts, corresponding in number with the representatives to which it may be entitled; which districts shall be formed of contiguous counties, and be compact. Each district shall contain, as nearly as may be, an equal number of population, to be determined according to the rule prescribed in the constitution of the United States.

ARTICLE II: THE STATE

Section 1. The State

The territory of the following counties, formerly parts of the commonwealth of Virginia, shall constitute and form the state of West Virginia, viz:

The counties of Barbour, Berkeley, Boone, Braxton, Brooke, Cabell, Calhoun, Clay, Doddridge, Fayette, Gilmer, Grant, Greenbrier, Hampshire, Hancock, Hardy, Harrison, Jackson, Jefferson, Kanawha, Lewis, Lincoln, Logan, Marion, Marshall, Mason, McDowell, Mercer, Mineral, Monongalia, Monroe, Morgan, Nicholas, Ohio, Pendleton, Pleasants, Pocahontas, Preston, Putnam, Raleigh, Randolph, Ritchie, Roane, Summers, Taylor, Tucker, Tyler, Upshur, Wayne, Webster, Wetzel, Wirt, Wood and Wyoming. The state of West Virginia includes the bed, bank and shores of the Ohio River, and so much of the Big Sandy River as was formerly included in the commonwealth of Virginia; and all territorial rights and property in, and jurisdiction over, the same, heretofore reserved by, and vested in, the commonwealth of Virginia, are vested in and shall hereafter be exercised by the state of West Virginia. And such parts of the said beds, banks and shores as lie opposite, and adjoining the several counties of this state, shall form parts of said several counties respectively.

Section 2. Powers of Government in Citizens

The powers of government reside in all the citizens of the state, and can be rightfully exercised only in accordance with their will and appointment.

Section 3. Requisites of Citizenship

All persons residing in this state, born, or naturalized in the United States, and subject to the jurisdiction thereof, shall be citizens of this state.

Section 4. Equal Representation

Every citizen shall be entitled to equal representation in the government, and, in all apportionments of representation, equality of numbers of those entitled thereto, shall as far as practicable, be preserved.

Section 5. Provisions Regarding Property

No distinction shall be made between resident aliens and citizens, as to the acquisition, tenure, disposition or descent of property.

Section 6. Treason, What Constitutes/Penalty

Treason against the state shall consist only in levying war against it, or in adhering to its enemies, giving them aid and comfort. No person shall be convicted of treason, unless on the testimony of two witnesses to the same overt act, or on confession in open court. Treason shall be punished according to the character of the acts committed, by the infliction of one, or more, of the penalties of death, imprisonment or fine, as may be prescribed by law.

Section 7. "Montani Semper Liberi" State Seal

The present seal of the state, with its motto, "Montani Semper Liberi," shall be the great seal of the state of West Virginia, and shall be kept by the secretary of state, to be used by him officially, as directed by law.

Section 8. Writs, Commissions, Official Bonds/Indictments

Writs, grants and commissions, issued under the authority of this state, shall run in the name of, and official bonds shall be made payable to the state of West Virginia. Indictments shall conclude, "Against the peace and dignity of the state."

ARTICLE III: BILL OF RIGHTS

Section 1. Bill of Rights

All men are, by nature, equally free and independent, and have certain inherent rights, of which, when they enter into a state of society, they cannot, by any compact, deprive or divest their posterity, namely: The enjoyment of life and liberty, with the means of acquiring and possessing property, and of pursuing and obtaining happiness and safety.

Section 2. Magistrates Servants of People

All power is vested in, and consequently derived from, the people. Magistrates are their trustees and servants, and at all times amenable to them.

Section 3. Rights Reserved to People

Government is instituted for the common benefit, protection and security of the people, nation or community. Of all its various forms that is the best, which is capable of producing the greatest degree of happiness and safety, and is most effectually secured against the danger of maladministration; and when any government shall be found inadequate or contrary to these purposes, a majority of the community has an indubitable, inalienable, and indefeasible right to reform, alter or abolish it in such manner as shall be judged most conducive to the public weal.

Section 4. Writ of Habeas Corpus

The privilege of the writ of habeas corpus shall not be suspended. No person shall be held to answer for treason, felony or other crime, not cognizable by a justice, unless on presentment or indictment of a grand jury. No bill of attainder, ex post facto law, or law impairing the obligation of a contract, shall be passed.

Section 5. Excessive Bail Not Required

Excessive bail shall not be required, nor excessive fines imposed, nor cruel and unusual punishment inflicted. Penalties shall be proportioned to the character and degree of the offence. No person shall be transported out of, or forced to leave the state for any offence committed within the same; nor shall any person, in any criminal case, be compelled to be a witness against himself, or be twice put in jeopardy of life or liberty for the same offence.

Section 6. Unreasonable Searches and Seizures Prohibited

The rights of the citizens to be secure in their houses, persons, papers and effects, against unreasonable searches and seizures, shall not be violated. No warrant shall issue except upon probable cause, supported by oath or affirmation, particularly describing the place to be searched, or the person or thing to be seized.

Section 7. Freedom of Speech and Press Guaranteed

No law abridging the freedom of speech, or of the press, shall be passed; but the Legislature may, by suitable penalties, restrain the publication or sale of obscene books, papers, or pictures, and provide for the punishment of libel, and defamation of character, and for the recovery, in civil actions, by the aggrieved party, of suitable damages for such libel, or defamation.

Section 8. Relating To Civil Suits for Libel

In prosecutions and civil suits for libel, the truth may be given in evidence; and if it shall appear to the jury, that the matter charged as libelous is true, and was published with good motives, and for justifiable ends, the verdict shall be for the defendant.

Section 9. Private Property, How Taken

Private property shall not be taken or damaged for public use, without just compensation; nor shall the same be taken by any company, incorporated for the purposes of internal improvement, until just compensation shall have been paid, or secured to be paid, to the owner; and when private property shall be taken, or damaged for public use, or for the use of such corporation, the compensation to the owner shall be ascertained in such manner as may be prescribed by general law: Provided, That when required by either of the parties, such compensation shall be ascertained by an impartial jury of twelve freeholders.

Section 10. Safeguards For Life, Liberty and Property

No person shall be deprived of life, liberty, or property, without due process of law, and the judgment of his peers.

Section 11. Political Tests Condemned

Political tests, requiring persons, as a prerequisite to the enjoyment of their civil and political rights, to purge themselves by their own oaths, of past alleged offences, are repugnant to the principles of free government, and are cruel and oppressive. No religious or political test oath shall be required as a prerequisite or qualification to vote, serve as a juror, sue, plead, appeal, or pursue any profession or employment. Nor shall any person be deprived by law, of any right, or privilege, because of any act done prior to the passage of such law.

Section 12. Military Subordinate To Civil Power

Standing armies, in time of peace, should be avoided as dangerous to liberty. The military shall be subordinate to the civil power; and no citizen, unless engaged in the military service of the state, shall be tried or punished by any military court, for any offence that is cognizable by the civil courts of the state. No soldier shall, in time of peace, be quartered in any house, without consent of the owner; nor in time of war, except in the manner to be prescribed by law.

Section 13. Right of Jury Trial

In suits at common law, where the value in controversy exceeds twenty dollars exclusive of interest and costs, the right of trial by jury, if required by either party, shall be preserved; and in such suit in a court of limited jurisdiction a jury shall consist of six persons. No fact tried by a jury shall be otherwise reexamined in any case than according to the rule of court or law.

Section 14. Trials of Crimes/Provisions in Interest of Accused

Trials of crimes, and of misdemeanors, unless herein otherwise provided, shall be by a jury of twelve men, public, without unreasonable delay, and in the county where the alleged offence was committed, unless upon petition of the accused, and for good cause shown, it is removed to some other county. In all such trials, the accused shall be fully and plainly informed of the character and cause of the accusation, and be confronted with the witnesses against him, and shall have the assistance of counsel, and a reasonable time to prepare for his defence; and there shall be awarded to him compulsory process for obtaining witnesses in his favor.

Section 15. Religious Freedom Guaranteed

No man shall be compelled to frequent or support any religious worship, place or ministry whatsoever; nor shall any man be enforced, restrained, molested or burthened, in his body or goods, or otherwise suffer, on account of his religious opinions or belief, but all men shall be free to profess and by argument, to maintain their opinions in matters of religion; and the same shall, in nowise, affect, diminish or enlarge their civil capacities; and the Legislature shall not prescribe any religious test whatever, or confer any peculiar privileges or advantages on any sect or denomination, or pass any law requiring or authorizing any religious society, or the people of any district within this state, to levy on themselves, or others, any tax for the erection or repair of any house for public worship, or for the support of any church or ministry, but it shall be left free for every person to select his religious instructor, and to make for his support, such private contracts as he shall please.

Section 15a. Voluntary Contemplation, Meditation or Prayer iin Schools

Public schools shall provide a designated brief time at the beginning of each school day for any student desiring to exercise their right to personal and private contemplation, meditation or prayer. No student of a public school may be denied the right to personal and private contemplation, meditation or prayer nor shall any student be required or encouraged to engage in any given contemplation, meditation or prayer as a part of the school curriculum.

Section 16. Right Of Public Assembly Held Inviolate

The right of the people to assemble in a peaceable manner, to consult for the common good, to instruct their representatives, or to apply for redress of grievances, shall be held inviolate.

Section 17. Courts Open To All/Justice Administered Speedily

The courts of this state shall be open, and every person, for an injury done to him, in his person, property or reputation, shall have remedy by due course of law; and justice shall be administered without sale, denial or delay.

Section 18. Conviction not to Work Corruption of Blood or Forfeiture

No conviction shall work corruption of blood or forfeiture of estate.

Section 19. Hereditary Emoluments, Etc., Provided Against

No hereditary emoluments, honors or privileges shall ever be granted or conferred in this state.

Section 20. Preservation of Free Government

Free government and the blessings of liberty can be preserved to any people only by a firm adherence to justice, moderation, temperance, frugality and virtue, and by a frequent recurrence to fundamental principles.

Section 21. Jury Service for Women

Regardless of sex all persons, who are otherwise qualified, shall be eligible to serve as petit jurors, in both civil and criminal cases, as grand jurors and as coroner's jurors.

Section 22. Right to Keep and Bear Arms

A person has the right to keep and bear arms for the defense of self, family, home anc state, and for lawful hunting and recreational use.

ARTICLE IV: ELECTION AND OFFICERS

Section 1. Election and Officers

The citizens of the state shall be entitled to vote at all elections held within the counties in which they respectively reside; but no person who is a minor, or who has been declared mentally incompetent by a court of competent jurisdiction, or who is under conviction of treason, felony or bribery in an election, or who has not been a resident of the state and of the county in which he offers to vote, for thirty days next preceding such offer, shall be permitted to vote while such disability continues; but no person in the military, naval or marine service of the United States shall be deemed a resident of this state by reason of being stationed therein.

Section 2. Mode of Voting by Ballot

In all elections by the people, the mode of voting shall be by ballot; but the voter shall be left free to vote by either open, sealed or secret ballot, as he may elect.
Section 3. Voter not subject to arrest on civil process.
No voter, during the continuance of an election at which he is entitled to vote, or during the time necessary and convenient for going to and returning from the same, shall be subject to arrest upon civil process, or be compelled to attend any court, or judicial proceeding, as suitor, juror or witness; or to work upon the public roads; or, except in time of war or public danger, to render military service.

Section 4. Persons Entitled to Hold Office/Age Requirements

No person, except citizens entitled to vote, shall be elected or appointed to any state, county or municipal office; but the governor and judges must have attained the age of thirty, and the attorney general and senators the age of twenty-five years, at the beginning of their respective terms of service; and must have been citizens of the state for five years next preceding their election or appointment, or be citizens at the time this constitution goes into operation.

Section 5. Oath or Affirmation to Support the Constitution

Every person elected or appointed to any office, before proceeding to exercise the authority, or discharge the duties thereof, shall make oath or affirmation that he will support the constitution of the United States and the constitution of this state, and that he will faithfully discharge the duties of his said office to the best of his skill and judgment; and no other oath, declaration, or test shall be required as a qualification, unless herein otherwise provided.

Section 6. Provisions for Removal of Officials

All officers elected or appointed under this constitution, may, unless in cases herein otherwise provided for, be removed from office for official misconduct, incompetence, neglect of duty, or gross immorality, in such manner as may be prescribed by general laws, and unless so removed they shall continue to discharge the duties of their respective offices until their successors are elected, or appointed and qualified.

Section 7. General Elections, When Held/Terms of Officials

The general elections of state and county officers, and of members of the Legislature, shall be held on the Tuesday next after the first Monday in November, until otherwise provided by law. The terms of such officers, not elected, or appointed to fill a vacancy, shall, unless herein otherwise provided, begin on the first day of January; and of the members of the Legislature, on the first day of December next succeeding their election. Elections to fill vacancies, shall be for the unexpired term. When vacancies occur prior to any general election, they shall be filled by appointments, in such manner as may be prescribed herein, or by general law, which appointments shall expire at such time after the next general election as the person so elected to fill such vacancy shall be qualified.

Section 8. Further Provisions Regarding State's Officers and Agents

The Legislature, in cases not provided for in this constitution, shall prescribe, by general laws, the terms of office, powers, duties and compensation of all public officers and agents, and the manner in which they shall be elected, appointed and removed.

Section 9. Impeachment of Officials

Any officer of the state may be impeached for maladministration, corruption, incompetency, gross immorality, neglect of duty, or any high crime or misdemeanor. The House of Delegates shall have the sole power of impeachment. The Senate shall have the sole power to try impeachments and no person shall be convicted without the concurrence of two thirds of the members elected thereto. When sitting as a court of impeachment, the president of the supreme court of appeals, or, if from any cause it be improper for him to act, then any other judge of that court, to be designated by it, shall preside; and the senators shall be on oath or affirmation, to do justice according to law and evidence. Judgment in cases of impeachment shall not extend further than to removal from office, and disqualification to hold any office of honor, trust or profit, under the state; but the party convicted shall be liable to indictment, trial, judgment, and punishment according to law. The Senate may sit during the recess of the Legislature for the trial of impeachments.

Section 10. Fighting of Duels Prohibited

Any citizen of this state, who shall, after the adoption of this constitution, either in or out of the state, fight a duel with deadly weapons, or send or accept a challenge so to do, or who shall act as a second or knowingly aid or assist in such duel, shall, ever thereafter, be incapable of holding any office of honor, trust or profit in this state.

Section 11. Safeguards for Ballots

The Legislature shall prescribe the manner of conducting and making returns of elections, and of determining contested elections; and shall pass such laws as may be necessary and proper to prevent intimidation, disorder or violence at the polls, and corruption or fraud in voting, counting the vote, ascertaining or declaring the result, or fraud in any manner upon the ballot.

Section 12. Registration Laws Provided For

The Legislature shall enact proper laws for the registration of all qualified voters in this state.

ARTICLE V: DIVISION OF POWER

Section 1. Division of Powers

The legislative, executive and judicial departments shall be separate and distinct, so that neither shall exercise the powers properly belonging to either of the others; nor shall any person exercise the powers of more than one of them at the same time, except that justices of the peace shall be eligible to the Legislature.

ARTICLE VI: THE LEGISLATURE

Section 1. The Legislature

The legislative power shall be vested in a Senate and House of Delegates. The style of their acts shall be, "Be it enacted by the Legislature of West Virginia."

Section 2. Composition of Senate and House of Delegates

The Senate shall be composed of twenty-four, and the House of Delegates of sixty-five members, subject to be increased according to the provisions hereinafter contained.

Section 3. Senators and Delegates/Terms of Office

Senators shall be elected for the term of four years, and delegates for the term of two years. The senators first elected, shall divide themselves into two classes, one senator from every district being assigned to each class; and of these classes, the first to be designated by lot in such manner as the Senate may determine, shall hold their seats for two years and the second for four years, so that after the first election, one half of the senators shall be elected biennially.

Section 4. Division of State into Senatorial Districts

For the election of senators, the state shall be divided into twelve senatorial districts, which number shall not be diminished, but may be increased as hereinafter provided. Every district shall elect two senators, but, where the district is composed of more than one county, both shall not be chosen from the same county. The districts shall be compact, formed of contiguous territory, bounded by county lines, and, as nearly as practicable, equal in population, to be ascertained by the census of the United States. After every such census, the Legislature shall alter the senatorial districts, so far as may be necessary to make them conform to the foregoing provision.

Section 5. Senatorial Districts Designated

Until the senatorial districts shall be altered by the Legislature as herein prescribed, the counties of Hancock, Brooke and Ohio, shall constitute the first senatorial district; Marshall, Wetzel and Marion, the second; Ritchie, Doddridge, Harrison, Gilmer and Calhoun, the third; Tyler, Pleasants, Wood and Wirt, the fourth; Jackson, Mason, Putnam and Roane, the fifth; Kanawha, Clay, Nicholas, Braxton and Webster, the sixth; Cabell, Wayne, Lincoln, Boone, Logan, Wyoming, McDowell and Mercer, the seventh; Monroe, Greenbrier, Summers, Pocahontas, Fayette and Raleigh, the eighth; Lewis, Randolph, Upshur, Barbour, Taylor and Tucker, the ninth; Preston and Monongalia, the tenth; Hampshire, Mineral, Hardy, Grant and Pendleton, the eleventh; Berkeley, Morgan and Jefferson, the twelfth.

Section 6. Provision for Delegate Representation

For the election of delegates, every county containing a population of less than three fifths of the ratio of representation for the House of Delegates, shall, at each apportionment, be attached to some contiguous county or counties, to form a delegate district.

Section 7. After Census, Delegate Apportionment

After every census the delegates shall be apportioned as follows: The ratio of representation for the House of Delegates shall be ascertained by dividing the whole population of the state by the number of which the House is to consist and rejecting the fraction of a unit, if any, resulting from such division. Dividing the population of every delegate district, and of every county not included in a delegate district, by the ratio thus ascertained, there shall be assigned to each a number of delegates equal to the quotient obtained by this division, excluding the fractional remainder. The additional delegates necessary to make up the number of which the House is to consist, shall then be assigned to those delegate districts, and counties not included in a delegate district, which would otherwise have the largest fractions unrepresented; but every delegate district and county not included in a delegate district, shall be entitled to at least one delegate.

Section 8. Designation of delegate districts

Until a new apportionment shall be declared, the counties of Pleasants and Wood shall form the first delegate district, and elect three delegates; Ritchie and Calhoun, the second, and elect two delegates; Barbour, Harrison and Taylor, the third, and elect one delegate; Randolph and Tucker, the fourth, and elect one delegate; Nicholas, Clay and Webster, the fifth, and elect one delegate; McDowell and Wyoming, the sixth, and elect one delegate.

Section 9. Further apportionments

Until a new apportionment shall be declared, the apportionment of delegates to the counties not included in delegate districts, and to Barbour, Harrison and Taylor counties, embraced in such district, shall be as follows:

To Barbour, Boone, Braxton, Brooke, Cabell, Doddridge, Fayette, Hampshire, Hancock, Jackson, Lewis, Logan, Greenbrier, Monroe, Mercer, Mineral, Morgan, Grant, Hardy, Lincoln, Pendleton, Putnam, Roane, Gilmer, Taylor, Tyler, Upshur, Wayne, Wetzel, Wirt, Pocahontas, Summers and Raleigh counties, one delegate each.

To Berkeley, Harrison, Jefferson, Marion, Marshall, Mason, Monongalia and Preston counties, two delegates each.

To Kanawha county, three delegates.

To Ohio county, four delegates.

Section 10. Arrangement of Senatorial and Delegate Districts

The arrangement of the senatorial and delegate districts, and apportionment of delegates, shall hereafter be declared by law, as soon as possible after each succeeding census, taken by authority of the United States. When so declared they shall apply to the first general election for members of the Legislature, to be thereafter held, and shall continue in force unchanged, until such districts shall be altered, and delegates apportioned, under the succeeding census.

Section 11. Additional Territory may be Admitted into State

Additional territory may be admitted into, and become part of this state, with the consent of the Legislature and a majority of the qualified voters of the state, voting on the question. And in such case provision shall be made by law for the representation thereof in the Senate and House of Delegates, in conformity with the principles set forth in this constitution. And the number of members of which each house of the Legislature is to consist, shall thereafter be increased by the representation assigned to such additional territory.

Section 12. Senators and Delegates Required to be Residents of Districts

No person shall be a senator or delegate who has not for one year next preceding his election, been a resident within the district or county from which he is elected; and if a senator or delegate remove from the district or county for which he was elected, his seat shall be thereby vacated.

Section 13. Eligibility to Seat in Legislature

No person holding any other lucrative office or employment under this state, the United States, or any foreign government; no member of Congress; and no person who is sheriff, constable, or clerk of any court of record, shall be eligible to a seat in the

Legislature.

Section 14. Bribery Conviction Forfeits Eligibility

No person who has been, or hereafter shall be convicted of bribery, perjury, or other infamous crimes, shall be eligible to a seat in the Legislature. No person who may have collected or been entrusted with public money, whether state, county, township, district, or other municipal organization, shall be eligible to the Legislature, or to any office of honor, trust, or profit in this state, until he shall have duly accounted for and paid over such money according to law.

Section 15. Senators and Delegates not to Hold Civil Office for Profit

No senator or delegate, during the term for which he shall have been elected, shall be elected or appointed to any civil office of profit under this state, which has been created, or the emoluments of which have been increased during such term, except offices to be filled by election by the people. Nor shall any member of the Legislature be interested, directly or indirectly, in any contract with the state, or any county thereof, authorized by any law passed during the term for which he shall have been elected.

Section 16. Oath of Senators And Delegates

Members of the Legislature, before they enter upon their duties, shall take and subscribe the following oath or affirmation: "I do solemnly swear (or affirm) that I will support the Constitution of the United States, and the Constitution of the State of West Virginia, and faithfully discharge the duties of Senator (or Delegate) according to the best of my ability"; and they shall also take this further oath, to wit: "I will not accept or receive, directly or indirectly, any money or other valuable thing, from any corporation, company, or person for any vote or influence I may give or withhold, as Senator (or Delegate) on any bill, resolution or appropriation, or for any act I may do or perform as Senator (or Delegate)." These oaths shall be administered in the hall of the house to which the member is elected, by a judge of the supreme court of appeals, or of a circuit court, or by any other person authorized by law to administer an oath; and the secretary of state shall record and file said oaths subscribed by each member; and no other oath or declaration shall be required as a qualification. Any member who shall refuse to take the oath herein prescribed, shall forfeit his seat; and any member who shall be convicted of having violated the oath last above required to be taken, shall forfeit his seat and be disqualified thereafter from holding any office of profit or trust in this state.

Section 17. Members of Legislature Privileged From Civil Arrest

Members of the Legislature shall, in all cases except treason, felony, and breach of the peace, be privileged from arrest during the session, and for ten days before and after the same; and for words spoken in debate, or any report, motion or proposition made in either house, a member shall not be questioned in any other place.

Section 18. Time and Place of Assembly of Legislature

The Legislature shall assemble annually at the seat of government, and not oftener unless convened by the governor. Regular sessions of the Legislature shall commence on the second Wednesday of January of each year. Upon the convening of the Legislature in each odd-numbered year, each house shall proceed to organize by the election of its officers for two-year terms and both houses shall then in joint assembly open and publish the election returns delivered to the Legislature as prescribed by other provisions of this constitution and by general law. When all of these matters have been completed in the year one thousand nine hundred seventy-three and every fourth year thereafter, the Legislature shall adjourn until the second Wednesday of February following. Notwithstanding the provisions of section fifty-one of this article and any other provisions of this constitution, on and after the effective date hereof, there shall be submitted by the governor to the Legislature, on the second Wednesday of February in the year one thousand nine hundred seventy-three and every fourth year thereafter, and on the second Wednesday of January of all other years, unless a later time in any year be fixed by the Legislature, a budget for the next ensuing fiscal year and a bill for the proposed appropriations of such budget.

Section 19. Convening of Legislature by Governor

The governor may convene the Legislature by proclamation whenever, in his opinion, the public safety or welfare shall require it. It shall be his duty to convene it, on application in writing, of three fifths of the members elected to each house.

Section 20. Seat of Government

The seat of government shall be at Charleston, until otherwise provided by law.

Section 21. Provisions for Assembling of Legislature Other Than at the Seat of Government

The governor may convene the Legislature at another place, when, in his opinion, it can not safely assemble at the seat of government, and the Legislature may, when in session, adjourn to some other place, when in its opinion, the public safety or welfare, or the safety of the members, or their health, shall require it.

Section 22. Length of Legislative Session

The regular session of the Legislature held in the year one thousand nine hundred seventy-three and every fourth year thereafter shall, in addition to the meeting days preceding the adjournment provided for in section eighteen of this article, not exceed sixty calendar days computed from and including the second Wednesday of February, and the regular session held in all other years shall not exceed sixty calendar days computed from and including the second Wednesday of January. Any regular session may be extended by a concurrent resolution adopted by a two-thirds vote of the members elected to each house determined by yeas and nays and entered on the journals.

Section 23. Concerning Adjournment

Neither house shall, during the session, adjourn for more than three days, without the consent of the other. Nor shall either, without such consent, adjourn to any other place than that in which the Legislature is sitting.

Section 24. Rules Governing Legislative Proceedings

A majority of the members elected to each house of the Legislature shall constitute a quorum. But a smaller number may adjourn from day to day, and shall be authorized to compel the attendance of absent members, as each house may provide. Each house shall determine the rules of its proceedings and be the judge of the elections, returns and qualifications of its own members. The Senate shall choose, from its own body, a president; and the House of Delegates, from its own body, a speaker. Each house shall appoint its own officers, and remove them at pleasure. The oldest delegate in point of continuous service present at the assembly of the Legislature at which officers thereof are to be selected, and if there be two or more such delegates with equal continuous service the one agreed upon by such delegates or chosen by such delegates by lot, shall call the House to order, and preside over it until the speaker thereof shall have been chosen, and have taken his seat. The oldest member of the Senate in point of continuous service present at the assembly of the Legislature at which officers thereof are to be selected, and if there be two or more such members with equal continuous service the one agreed upon by such members or chosen by such members by lot, shall call the Senate to order, and preside over the same until a president of the Senate shall have been chosen, and have taken his seat.

Section 25. Authority to Punish Members

Each house may punish its own members for disorderly behavior, and with the concurrence of two thirds of the members elected thereto, expel a member, but not twice for the same offence.

Section 26. Provisions for Undisturbed Transaction of Business

Each house shall have power to provide for its own safety, and the undisturbed transaction of its business, and may punish, by imprisonment, any person not a member, for disrespectful behavior in its presence; for obstructing any of its proceedings, or any of its officers in the discharge of his duties, or for any assault, threat or abuse of a member, for words spoken in debate. But such imprisonment shall not extend beyond the termination of the session, and shall not prevent the punishment of any offence, by the ordinary course of law.

Section 27. Accounting for State Moneys

Laws shall be enacted and enforced, by suitable provisions and penalties, requiring sheriffs, and all other officers, whether state, county, district or municipal, who shall collect or receive, or whose official duty it is, or shall be, to collect, receive, hold or pay out any money belonging to, or which is, or shall be, for the use of the state or of any county, district, or municipal corporation, to make annual account and settlement therefor. Such settlement, when made, shall be subject to exceptions, and take such direction, and have only such force and effect, as may be provided by law; but in all cases such settlement shall be recorded, and be open to the examination of the people at such convenient place or places as may be appointed by law.

Section 28. Origination of Bills

Bills and resolutions may originate in either house, but may be passed, amended or rejected by the other.

Section 29. Requirement for Reading of Bills

No bill shall become a law until it has been fully and distinctly read, on three different days, in each house, unless in case of urgency, by a vote of four fifths of the members present, taken by yeas and nays on each bill, this rule be dispensed with: Provided, in all cases, that an engrossed bill shall be fully and distinctly read in each house.

Section 30. Acts to Embrace But One Object/Time of Effect

No act hereafter passed shall embrace more than one object, and that shall be expressed in the title. But if any object shall be embraced in an act which is not so expressed, the act shall be void only as to so much thereof, as shall not be so expressed, and no law shall be revived, or amended, by reference to its title only; but the law revived, or the section amended, shall be inserted at large, in the new act. And no act of the Legislature, except such as may be passed at the first session under this constitution, shall take effect until the expiration of ninety days after its passage, unless the Legislature shall by a vote of two thirds of the members elected to each house, taken by yeas and nays, otherwise direct.

Section 31. How Bills may be Amended

When a bill or joint resolution, passed by one house, shall be amended by the other, the question on agreeing to the bill, or joint resolution, as amended, shall be again voted on, by yeas and nays, in the house by which it was originally passed, and the result entered upon its journals; in all such cases, the affirmative vote of a majority of all the members elected to such house shall be necessary.

Section 32. "Majority" Defined

Whenever the words, "a majority of the members elected to either house of the Legislature," or words of like import, are used in this constitution, they shall be construed to mean a majority of the whole number of members to which each house is, at the time, entitled, under the apportionment of representation, established by the provisions of this constitution.

Section 33. Compensation and Expenses of Members

Members of the Legislature shall receive such compensation in connection with the performance of their respective duties as members of the Legislature and such allowances for travel and other expenses in connection therewith as shall be

(1) established in a resolution submitted to the Legislature by the Citizens Legislative Compensation Commission hereinafter created, and

(2) thereafter enacted into general law by the Legislature at a regular session thereof, subject to such requirements and conditions as shall be prescribed in such general law. The Legislature may in any such general law reduce but shall not increase any item of compensation or expense allowance established in such resolution. All voting on the floor of both houses on the question of passage of any such general law shall be by yeas and nays to be entered on the journals.

The Citizens Legislative Compensation Commission is hereby created. It shall be composed of seven members who have been residents of this state for at least ten years prior to the date of appointment, to be appointed by the governor within twenty days after ratification of this amendment, no more than four of whom shall be members of the same political party. The members shall be broadly representative of the public at large. Members of the Legislature and officers and employees of the state or of any county, municipality or other governmental unit of the state shall not be eligible for appointment to or to serve as members of the commission. Each member of the commission shall serve for a term of seven years, except of the members first appointed, one member shall be appointed for a term of one year, and one each for terms ending two, three, four, five, six and seven years after the date of appointment. As the term of each member first appointed expires, a successor shall be appointed for a seven-year term. Any member may be reappointed for any number of terms, and any vacancy shall be filled by the governor for the unexpired term. Any member of the commission may be removed by the governor prior to the expiration of such member's term for official misconduct, incompetency or neglect of duty. The governor shall designate one member of the commission as chairman. The members of the commission shall serve without compensation, but shall be entitled to be reimbursed for all reasonable and necessary expenses actually incurred in the performance of their duties as such members.

The commission shall meet as often as may be necessary and shall within fifteen days after the beginning of the regular session of the Legislature in the year one thousand nine hundred seventy-one and within fifteen days after the beginning of the regular session in each fourth year thereafter submit by resolution to the Legislature its determination of compensation and expense allowances, which resolution must be concurred in by at least four members of the commission.

Notwithstanding any other provision of this constitution, such compensation and expense allowances as may be provided for by any such general law shall be paid on and after the effective date of such general law. Until the first such general law becomes effective, the provisions of this section in effect immediately prior to the ratification of this amendment shall continue to govern.

Section 34. Distribution of Laws and Journals Provided for, Contracts for Printing

The Legislature shall provide by law that the fuel, stationery and printing paper, furnished for the use of the state; the copying, printing, binding and distributing the laws and journals; and all other printing ordered by the Legislature, shall be let by contract to the lowest responsible bidder, bidding under a maximum price to be fixed by the Legislature; and no member or officer thereof, or officer of the state, shall be interested, directly or indirectly, in such contract, but all such contracts shall be subject to the approval of the governor, and in case of his disapproval of any such contract, there shall be a reletting of the same in such manner as may be prescribed by law.

Section 35. State not to be Made Defendant in any Court

The state of West Virginia shall never be made defendant in any court of law or equity, except the state of West Virginia, including any subdivision thereof, or any municipality therein, or any officer, agent, or employee thereof, may be made defendant in any garnishment or attachment proceeding, as garnishee or suggestee.

Section 36. Lotteries; Bingo; Raffles; County Option

The Legislature shall have no power to authorize lotteries or gift enterprises for any purpose, and shall pass laws to prohibit the sale of lottery or gift enterprise tickets in this State; except that the Legislature may authorize lotteries which are regulated, controlled, owned and operated by the State of West Virginia in the manner provided by general law, either separately by this state or jointly or in cooperation with one or more other states and may authorize state-regulated bingo games and raffles for the purpose of raising money by charitable or public service organizations or by the State Fair of West Virginia for charitable or public service purposes: Provided, That each county may disapprove the holding of bingo games and raffles within that county at a regular, primary or special election but once having disapproved such activity, may thereafter authorize the holding of bingo games and raffles, by majority vote at a regular, primary or special election held not sooner than five years after the election resulting in disapproval; that all proceeds from the bingo games and raffles be used for the purpose of supporting charitable or public service purposes; and that the Legislature shall provide a means of regulating the bingo games and raffles so as to ensure that only charitable or public service purposes are served by the conducting of the bingo games and raffles.

Section 37. Terms of Office not to be Extended After Election

No law shall be passed after the election of any public officer, which shall operate to extend the term of his office.

Section 38. Salaries of Officials Cannot be Increased During Official Terms

No extra compensation shall be granted or allowed to any public officer, agent, servant or contractor, after the services shall have been rendered or the contract made; nor shall any Legislature authorize the payment of any claim or part thereof, hereafter created against the state, under any agreement or contract made, without express authority of law; and all such unauthorized agreements shall be null and void. Nor shall the salary of any public officer be increased or diminished during his term of office, nor shall any such officer, or his or their sureties be released from any debt or liability due to the state: Provided, the Legislature may make appropriations for expenditures hereafter incurred in suppressing insurrection, or repelling invasion.

Section 39. Local Laws not to be Passed in Enumerated Cases

The Legislature shall not pass local or special laws in any of the following enumerated cases; that is to say, for

Granting divorces;

Laying out, opening, altering and working roads or highways; Vacating roads, town plats, streets, alleys and public grounds;

Locating, or changing county seats;

Regulating or changing county or district affairs;

Providing for the sale of church property, or property held for charitable uses;

Regulating the practice in courts of justice;

Incorporating cities, towns or villages, or amending the charter of any city, town or village, containing a population of less than two thousand;

Summoning or impaneling grand or petit juries;

The opening or conducting of any election, or designating the place of voting;

The sale and mortgage of real estate belonging to minors, or others under disability;

Chartering, licensing, or establishing ferries or toll bridges;

Remitting fines, penalties or forfeitures;

Changing the law of descent;

Regulating the rate of interest;

Authorizing deeds to be made for land sold for taxes;

Releasing taxes;

Releasing title to forfeited lands.

The Legislature shall provide, by general laws, for the foregoing and all other cases for which provision can be so made; and in no case shall a special act be passed, where a general law would be proper, and can be made applicable to the case, nor in any other case in which the courts have jurisdiction, and are competent to give the relief asked for.

Section 39a. Home Rule for Municipalities

No local or special law shall hereafter be passed incorporating cities, towns or villages, or amending their charters. The Legislature shall provide by general laws for the incorporation and government of cities, towns and villages, and shall classify such municipal corporations, upon the basis of population, into not less than two nor more than five classes. Such general laws shall restrict the powers of such cities, towns and villages to borrow money and contract debts, and shall limit the rate of taxes for municipal purposes, in accordance with section one, article ten of the constitution of the state of West Virginia. Under such general laws, the electors of each municipal corporation, wherein the population exceeds two thousand, shall have power and authority to frame, adopt and amend the charter of such corporation, or to amend an existing charter thereof, and through its legally constituted authority, may pass all laws and ordinances relating to its municipal affairs: Provided, That any such charter or amendment thereto, and any such law or ordinance so adopted, shall be invalid and void if inconsistent or in conflict with this constitution or the general laws of the state then in effect, or thereafter from time to time enacted.

Section 40. Limiting Powers of Court or Judge

The Legislature shall not confer upon any court, or judge, the power of appointment to office, further than the same is herein provided for.

Section 41. Each House to Keep Journal of Proceedings

Each house shall keep a journal of its proceedings, and cause the same to be published from time to time, and all bills and joint resolutions shall be described therein, as well by their title as their number, and the yeas and nays on any question, if called for by one tenth of those present shall be entered on the journal.

Section 42. Appropriation Bills to be Specific

Bills making appropriations for the pay of members and officers of the Legislature, and for salaries for the officers of the government, shall contain no provision on any other subject.

Section 43. Board Or Court Of Registration Of Voters Prohibited

The Legislature shall never authorize or establish any board or court of registration of voters.

Section 44. Election of Legislative, County and Municipal Officers

In all elections to office which may hereafter take place in the Legislature, or in any county, or municipal body, the vote shall be viva voce, and be entered on its journals.

Section 45. Bribery and Attempt to Bribe/Punishment

It shall be the duty of the Legislature, at its first session after the adoption of this constitution, to provide, by law, for the punishment by imprisonment in the penitentiary, of any person who shall bribe, or attempt to bribe, any executive or judicial officer of this state, or any member of the Legislature in order to influence him, in the performance of any of his official or public duties; and also to provide by law for the punishment by imprisonment in the penitentiary of any of said officers, or any member of the Legislature, who shall demand, or receive, from any corporation, company or person, any money, testimonial, or other valuable thing, for the performance of his official or public duties, or for refusing or failing to perform the same, or for any vote or influence a member of the Legislature may give or withhold as such member; and also to provide by law for compelling any person, so bribing or attempting to bribe, or so demanding or receiving a bribe, fee, reward, or testimonial, to testify against any person or persons, who may have committed any of said offences: Provided, That any person so compelled to testify, shall be exempted from trial and punishment for the offence of which he may have been guilty, and concerning which he is compelled to testify; and any person convicted of any of the offences specified in this section, shall, as a part of the punishment thereof, be forever disqualified from holding any office or position of honor, trust, or profit in this state.

Section 46. Manufacture and Sale of Liquor

The Legislature shall by appropriate legislation regulate the manufacture and sale of intoxicating liquors within the limits of this state, and any law authorizing the sale of such liquors shall forbid and penalize the consumption and the sale thereof for consumption in a saloon or other public place.

Section 47. Incorporation of Religious Denominations Prohibited

No charter of incorporation shall be granted to any church or religious denomination. Provisions may be made by general laws for securing the title to church property, and for the sale and transfer thereof, so that it shall be held, used, or transferred for the purposes of such church, or religious denomination.

Section 48. Homestead Exemption

Any husband or parent, residing in this state, or the infant children of deceased parents, may hold a homestead of the value of five thousand dollars, and personal property to the value of one thousand dollars, exempt from forced sale, subject to such regulations as shall be prescribed by law: Provided, That such homestead exemption shall in nowise affect debts or liabilities existing at the time of the adoption of this constitution and the increases in such homestead exemption provided by this amendment shall in nowise affect debts or liabilities existing at the time of the ratification of such amendment: Provided, however, That no property shall be exempt from sale for taxes due thereon, or for the payment of purchase money due upon said property, or for debts contracted for the erection of improvements thereon.

Section 49. Property of Married Woman

The Legislature shall pass such laws as may be necessary to protect the property of married women from the debts, liabilities and control of their husbands.

Section 50. Plan of Proportional Representation

The Legislature may provide for submitting to a vote of the people at the general election to be held in 1876, or at any general election thereafter, a plan or scheme of proportional representation in the Senate of this state; and if a majority of the votes cast at such election be in favor of the plan submitted to them, the Legislature shall, at its session succeeding such election, rearrange the senatorial districts in accordance with the plan so approved by the people.

Section 51. Budget and Supplementary Appropriation Bills

The Legislature shall not appropriate any money out of the treasury except in accordance with the provisions of this section.

Subsection A – Appropriation Bills

(1) Every appropriation bill shall be either a budget bill, or a supplementary appropriation bill, as hereinafter provided.

Subsection B – Budget Bills

(2) Within ten days after the convening of the regular session of the Legislature in odd-numbered years, unless such time shall be extended by the Legislature, and on the second Wednesday of January in even-numbered years, the governor shall submit to the Legislature a budget for the next ensuing fiscal year. The budget shall contain a complete plan of proposed expenditures and estimated revenues for the fiscal year and shall show the estimated surplus or deficit of revenues at the end of each fiscal year. Accompanying each budget shall be a statement showing:

(a) An estimate of the revenues and expenditures for the current fiscal year, including the actual revenues and actual expenditures to the extent available, and the revenues and expenditures for the next preceding fiscal year;

(b) the current assets, liabilities, reserves and surplus or deficit of the state;

(c) the debts and funds of the state;

(d) an estimate of the state's financial condition as of the beginning and end of the fiscal year covered by the budget;

(e) any explanation the governor may desire to make as to the important features of the budget and any suggestions as to methods for reduction or increase of the state's revenue.

(3) Each budget shall embrace an itemized estimate of the appropriations, in such form and detail as the governor shall determine or as may be prescribed by law:

(a) For the Legislature as certified to the governor in the manner hereinafter provided;

(b) for the executive department;

(c) for the judiciary department, as provided by law, certified to the governor by the auditor;

(d) for payment and discharge of the principal and interest of any debt of the state created in conformity with the constitution, and all laws enacted in pursuance thereof;

(e) for the salaries payable by the state under the constitution and laws of the state;

(f) for such other purposes as are set forth in the constitution and in laws made in pursuance thereof.

(4) The governor shall deliver to the presiding officer of each house the budget and a bill for all the proposed appropriations of the budget clearly itemized and classified, in such form and detail as the governor shall determine or as may be prescribed by law; and the presiding officer of each house shall promptly cause the bill to be introduced therein, and such bill shall be known as the "Budget Bill." The governor may, with the consent of the Legislature, before final action thereon by the Legislature, amend or supplement the budget to correct an oversight, or to provide funds contingent on passage of pending legislation, and in case of an emergency, he may deliver such an amendment or supplement to the presiding officers of both houses; and the amendment or supplement shall thereby become a part of the budget bill as an addition to the items of the bill or as a modification of or a substitute for any item of the bill the amendment or supplement may affect.

(5) The Legislature shall not amend the budget bill so as to create a deficit but may amend the bill by increasing or decreasing any item therein: Provided, That no item relating to the judiciary shall be decreased, and except as otherwise provided in this constitution, the salary or compensation of any public officer shall not be increased or decreased during his term of office: Provided further, That the Legislature shall not increase the estimate of revenue submitted in the budget without the approval of the governor.

(6) The governor and such representatives of the executive departments, boards, officers and commissions of the state expending or applying for state moneys as have been designated by the governor for this purpose, shall have the right, and when requested by either house of the Legislature it shall be their duty, to appear and be heard with respect to any budget bill, and to answer inquiries relative thereto.

Subsection C – Supplementary Appropriation Bills

(7) Neither house shall consider other appropriations until the budget bill has been finally acted upon by both houses, and no such other appropriations shall be valid except in accordance with the provisions following:

(a) Every such appropriation shall be embodied in a separate bill limited to some single work, object or purpose therein stated and called therein a supplementary appropriation bill;

(b) each supplementary appropriation bill shall provide the revenue necessary to pay the appropriation thereby made by a tax, direct or indirect, to be laid and collected as shall be directed in the bill unless it appears from such budget that there is sufficient revenue available.

Subsection D – General Provisions

(8) If the budget bill shall not have been finally acted upon by the Legislature three days before the expiration of its regular session, the governor shall issue a proclamation extending the session for such further period as may, in his judgment, be necessary for the passage of the bill; but no matter other than the bill shall be considered during such an extension of a session except a provision for the cost thereof.

(9) For the purpose of making up the budget, the governor shall have the power, and it shall be his duty, to require from the proper state officials, including herein all executive departments, all executive and administrative officers, bureaus, boards, commissions and agencies expending or supervising the expenditure of, and all institutions applying for state moneys and appropriations, such itemized estimates and other information, in such form and at such times as he shall direct. The estimates for the legislative department, certified by the presiding officer of each house, and for the judiciary, as provided by law, certified by the auditor, shall be transmitted to the governor in such form and at such times as he shall direct, and shall be included in the budget.

(10) The governor may provide for public hearings on all estimates and may require the attendance at such hearings of representatives of al agencies and all institutions applying for state moneys. After such public hearings he may, in his discretion, revise all estimates except those for the legislative and judiciary departments.

(11) Every budget bill or supplementary appropriation bill passed by a majority of the members elected to each house of the Legislature shall, before it becomes a law, be presented to the governor. The governor may veto the bill, or he may disapprove or reduce items or parts of items contained therein. If he approves he shall sign it and thereupon it shall become a law. The bill, items or parts thereof, disapproved or reduced by the governor, shall be returned with his objections to each house of the Legislature.

Each house shall enter the objections at large upon its journal and proceed to reconsider. If, after reconsideration, two thirds of the members elected to each house agree to pass the bill, or such items or parts thereof, as were disapproved or reduced, the bill, items or parts thereof, approved by two thirds of such members, shall become law, notwithstanding the objections of the governor. In all such cases, the vote of each house shall be

determined by yeas and nays to be entered on the journal.
A bill, item or part thereof, which is not returned by the governor within five days (Sundays excepted) after the bill has been presented to him shall become a law in like manner as if he had signed the bill, unless the Legislature, by adjournment, prevents such return, in which case it shall be filed in the office of the secretary of state, within five days after such adjournment, and shall become a law; or it shall be so filed within such five days with the objections of the governor, in which case it shall become law to the extent not disapproved by the governor.

(12) The Legislature may, from time to time, enact such laws, not inconsistent with this section, as may be necessary and proper to carry out its provisions.

(13) In the event of any inconsistency between any of the provisions of this section and any of the other provisions of the constitution, the provisions of this section shall prevail. But nothing herein shall be construed as preventing the governor from calling extraordinary sessions of the Legislature, as provided by section nineteen of this article, or as preventing the Legislature at such extraordinary sessions from considering any emergency appropriation or appropriations.

(14) If any item of any appropriation bill passed under the provisions of this section shall be held invalid upon any ground, such invalidity shall not affect the legality of the bill or of any other item of such bill or bills.

Section 52. Revenues Applicable to Roads

Revenue from gasoline and other motor fuel excise and license taxation, motor vehicle registration and license taxes, and all other revenue derived from motor vehicles or motor fuels shall, after the deduction of statutory refunds and cost of administration and collection authorized by legislative appropriation, be appropriated and used solely for construction, reconstruction, repair and maintenance of public highways, and also the payment of the interest and principal on all road bonds heretofore issued or which may be hereafter issued for the construction, reconstruction or improvement of public highways, and the payment of obligations incurred in the construction, reconstruction, repair and maintenance of public highways.

Section 53. Forestry Amendment

The Legislature may by general law define and classify forest lands and provide for cooperation by contract between the state and the owner in the planting, cultivation, protection, and harvesting thereof. Forest lands embraced in any such contract may be exempted from all taxation or be taxed in such manner, including the imposition of a severance tax or charge as trees are harvested, as the Legislature may from time to time provide. But any tax measured by valuation shall not exceed the aggregate rates authorized by section one of article ten of this constitution.

Section 54. Continuity of Government amendment

The Legislature of West Virginia, in order to insure continuity of state and local governmental operations in periods of emergency resulting from disasters caused by enemy attack, shall have the power and the immediate duty

(1) to provide for prompt and temporary succession to the powers and duties of public offices, of whatever nature and whether filled by election or appointment, the incumbents of which may become unavailable for carrying on the powers and duties of such officers, and

(2) to adopt such other measures as may be necessary and proper for insuring the continuity of governmental operations.

Section 55. Revenues and properties applicable to fish and wildlife conservation

Fees, moneys, interest or funds arising from the sales of all permits and licenses to hunt, trap, fish or otherwise hold or capture fish and wildlife resources and money reimbursed and granted by the federal government for fish and wildlife conservation shall be expended solely for the conservation, restoration, management, educational benefit, recreational use and scientific study of the state's fish and wildlife, including the purchases or other acquisition of property for said purposes and for the administration of the laws pertaining thereto and for no other purposes. In the event that any such properties or facilities are converted to uses other than those specified in this section and the conversion jeopardizes the availability of the receipt of federal funds by the state, the agency of the state responsible for the conservation of its fish and wildlife resources shall receive fair market compensation for the converted properties or facilities. Such compensation shall be expended only for the purposes specified in this section. All moneys shall be deposited within the state treasurer in the "license fund" and other specific funds created especially for fish and wildlife conservation and the public's use of fish and wildlife. Nothing in this section shall prevent the Legislature from reducing or increasing the amount of any permit or license to hunt, trap, fish or otherwise hold or capture fish or wildlife or to repeal or enact additional fees or requirements for the privilege of hunting, trapping, fishing or to otherwise hold or capture fish or wildlife.

Section 56. Revenues Applicable to Non-game Wildlife Resources in the State

Notwithstanding any provision of section fifty-two of article six of this Constitution, the legislature may, by general law, provide funding for conservation, restoration, management, educational benefit and recreational and scientific use of nongame wildlife resources in this state by providing a specialized nongame wildlife motor vehicle registration plate for motor vehicles registered in this state. The registration plate shall be issued on a voluntary basis pursuant to terms and conditions provided by general law for an additional fee above the basic registration and license fees and costs otherwise dedicated to the road fund. Any moneys collected from the issuance of these specialized registration plates in excess of those revenues otherwise dedicated to the road fund shall be deposited in a special revenue account in the state treasury and expended only in accordance with appropriations made by the Legislature as provided by general law for the conservation, restoration, management, educational benefit and recreational and scientific use of nongame wildlife resources in this state. All moneys collected which are in excess of the revenues otherwise dedicated to the road fund shall be deposited by the state treasurer in the "nongame wildlife fund" created especially for nongame wildlife resources in this state.

ARTICLE VII: EXECUTIVE DEPARTMENT

Section 1. Executive Department

The executive department shall consist of a governor, secretary of state, auditor, treasurer, commissioner of agriculture and attorney general, who shall be ex officio reporter of the court of appeals. Their terms of office shall be four years, and shall commence on the first Monday after the second Wednesday of January next after their election. They shall reside at the seat of government during their terms of office, keep there the public records, books and papers pertaining to their respective offices, and shall perform such duties as may be prescribed by law.

Section 2. Election

An election for governor, secretary of state, auditor, treasurer, commissioner of agriculture and attorney general shall be held at such times and places as may be prescribed by law.

Section 3. Certification of Election Returns/Contests

The returns of every election for the above named officers shall be sealed up and transmitted by the returning officers to the secretary of state, directed "to the speaker of the House of Delegates," who shall, immediately after the organization of the House, and before proceeding to business, open and publish the same, in the presence of a majority of each house of the Legislature, which shall for that purpose assemble in the hall of the House of Delegates. The person having the highest number of votes for either of said offices, shall be declared duly elected thereto; but if two or more have an equal and the highest number of votes for the same office, the Legislature shall, by joint vote, choose one of such persons for said office. Contested elections for the office of governor shall be determined by both houses of the Legislature by joint vote, in such manner as may be prescribed by law.

Section 4. Eligibility

None of the executive officers mentioned in this article shall hold any other office during the term of his service. A person who has been elected or who has served as governor during all or any part of two consecutive terms shall be ineligible for the office of governor during any part of the term immediately following the second of the two consecutive terms. The person holding the office of governor when this section is ratified shall not be prevented from holding the office of governor during the term immediately following the term he is then serving.

Section 5. Chief Executive/Powers

The chief executive power shall be vested in the governor, who shall take care that the laws be faithfully executed.

Section 6. Governor's Message

The governor shall at the commencement of each session, give to the Legislature information by message, of the condition of the state, and shall recommend such measures as he shall deem expedient. He shall accompany his message with a statement of all money received and paid out by him from any funds, subject to his order, with vouchers therefor; and at the commencement of each regular session, present estimates of the amount of money required by taxation for all purposes.

Section 7. Extraordinary Legislative Sessions

The governor may, on extraordinary occasions convene, at his own instance, the Legislature; but when so convened it shall enter upon no business except that stated in the proclamation by which it was called together.

Section 8. Governor to Nominate Certain Officers

The governor shall nominate, and by and with the advice and consent of the Senate, (a majority of all the senators elected concurring by yeas and nays) appoint all officers whose offices are established by this constitution, or shall be created by law, and whose appointment or election is not otherwise provided for; and no such officer shall be appointed or elected by the Legislature.

Section 9. Recess Vacancies/How Filled

In case of a vacancy, during the recess of the Senate, in any office which is not elective, the governor shall, by appointment, fill such vacancy, until the next meeting of the Senate, when he shall make a nomination for such office, and the person so nominated, when confirmed by the Senate, (a majority of all the senators elected concurring by yeas and nays) shall hold his office during the remainder of the term, and until his successor shall be appointed and qualified. No person, after being rejected by the Senate, shall be again nominated for the same office, during the same session, unless at the request of the Senate; nor shall such person be appointed to the same office during the recess of the Senate.

Section 10. Governor's Power of Removal

The governor shall have power to remove any officer whom he may appoint in case of incompetency, neglect of duty, gross immorality, or malfeasance in office; and he may declare his office vacant and fill the same as herein provided in other cases of vacancy.

Section 11. Executive May Remit Fines and Forfeitures

The governor shall have power to remit fines and penalties in such cases and under such regulations as may be prescribed by law; to commute capital punishment and, except where the prosecution has been carried on by the House of Delegates to grant reprieves and pardons after conviction; but he shall communicate to the Legislature at each session the particulars of every case of fine or penalty remitted, or punishment commuted and of reprieve or pardon granted, with his reasons therefor.

Section 12. Governor Commander-In-Chief of Military Forces

The governor shall be commander-in-chief of the military forces of the state, (except when they shall be called into the service of the United States) and may call out the same to execute the laws, suppress insurrection and repel invasion.

Section 13. Official Bond of State Officers

When any state officer has executed his official bond, the governor shall, for such causes and in such manner as the Legislature may direct, require of such officer reasonable additional security; and if the security is not given as required, his office shall be declared vacant, in such manner as may be provided by law.

Section 14. Governor's Approval or Disapproval of Bills Passed by the Legislature

Subject to the provisions of section fifteen of this article, every bill passed by the Legislature shall, before it becomes a law, be presented to the governor. If he approves, he shall sign it, and thereupon it shall become a law; but if not, he shall return it, with his objections, to the house in which it originated, which house shall enter the objections at large upon its journal, and may proceed to reconsider the returned bill. Notwithstanding the provisions of section fifty-one, article six of this constitution, any such bill may be reconsidered even if the Legislature is at the time in extended session for the sole purpose of considering the budget bill, as specified in said section fifty-one. If after any such reconsideration, a majority of the members elected to that house agree to pass the bill, it shall be sent, together with the objections of the governor to the other house, by which it may likewise be reconsidered, and if approved by a majority of the members elected to that house, it shall become a law, notwithstanding the objections of the governor. If upon any such reconsideration the bill is amended and reenacted, then it shall be again sent to the governor and he shall act upon it as if it were before him for the first time. In all cases, the vote of each house shall be determined by yeas and nays to be entered on the journal. Any bill which shall not be returned by the governor within five days, Sundays excepted, after it shall have been presented to him shall be a law, in the same manner as if he had signed it, unless the Legislature shall, by adjournment sine die, prevent its return, in which case it shall be filed with his objections in the office of the secretary of state within fifteen days, Sundays excepted, after such adjournment, or become a law.

Section 15. Governor's Approval or Disapproval of Bills Making Appropriations of Money

A bill passed by the Legislature making appropriations of money must be submitted to the governor for his approval or disapproval to the extent and only to the extent required by section fifty-one, article six of this constitution, and any provision therein contained as to such approval or disapproval shall govern and control as to any such bill.

Section 16. Vacancy in Governorship, How Filled

n case of the death, conviction or impeachment, failure to qualify, resignation, or other disability of the governor, the president of the Senate shall act as governor until the vacancy is filled, or the disability removed; and if the president of the Senate, for any of the above named causes, shall become incapable of performing the duties of governor, the same shall devolve upon the speaker of the House of Delegates; and in all other cases where there is no one to act as governor, one shall be chosen by joint vote of the Legislature. Whenever a vacancy shall occur in the office of governor before the first three years of the term shall have expired, a new election for governor shall take place to fill the vacancy.

Section 17. Vacancies in Other Executive Departments

If the office of secretary of state, auditor, treasurer, commissioner of agriculture or attorney general shall become vacant by death, resignation, or otherwise, it shall be the duty of the governor to fill the same by appointment, and the appointee shall hold his office until his successor shall be elected and qualified in such manner as may be prescribed by law. The subordinate officers of the executive department and the officers of all public institutions of the state shall keep an account of all moneys received or disbursed by them, respectively, from all sources, and for every service performed, and make a semiannual report thereof to the governor under oath or affirmation; and any officer who shall willfully make a false report shall be deemed guilty of perjury.

Section 18. Executive Heads to Make Reports

The subordinate officers of the executive department and the officers of all the public institutions of the state, shall, at least ten days preceding each regular session of the Legislature, severally report to the governor, who shall transmit such report to the Legislature; and the governor may at any time require information in writing, under oath, from the officers of his department, and all officers and managers of state institutions, upon any subject relating to the condition, management and expenses of their respective offices.

Section 19. Salaries of Officials

The officers named in this article shall receive for their services a salary to be established by law, which shall not be increased or diminished during their official terms, and they shall not, after the expirations of the terms of those in office at the adoption of this amendment, receive to their own use any fees, costs, perquisites of office or other compensation, and all fees that may hereafter be payable by law, for any service performed by any officer provided for in this article of the Constitution, shall be paid in advance into the state treasury.

ARTICLE VIII: JUDICIAL POWER

Section 1. Judicial Power

The judicial power of the state shall be vested solely in a supreme court of appeals and in the circuit courts, and in such intermediate appellate courts and magistrate courts as shall be hereafter established by the Legislature, and in the justices, judges and magistrates of such courts.

Section 2. Supreme Court of Appeals

The supreme court of appeals shall consist of five justices. A majority of the justices of the court shall constitute a quorum for the transaction of business.

The justices shall be elected by the voters of the state for a term of twelve years, unless sooner removed or retired as authorized in this article. The Legislature may prescribe by law whether the election of such justices is to be on a partisan or nonpartisan basis.

Provision shall be made by rules of the supreme court of appeals for the selection of a member of the court to serve as chief justice thereof. If the chief justice is temporarily disqualified or unable to serve, one of the justices of the court designated in accordance with the rules of the court shall serve temporarily in his stead.

When any justice is temporarily disqualified or unable to serve, the chief justice may assign a judge of a circuit court or of an intermediate appellate court to serve from time to time in his stead.

Section 3. Supreme Court of Appeals; Jurisdiction and Powers; Officers and Employees; Terms

The supreme court of appeals shall have original jurisdiction of proceedings in habeas corpus, mandamus, prohibition and certiorari.

The court shall have appellate jurisdiction in civil cases at law where the matter in controversy, exclusive of interest and costs, is of greater value or amount than three hundred dollars unless such value or amount is increased by the Legislature; in civil cases in equity; in controversies concerning the title or boundaries of land; in proceedings in quo warranto, habeas corpus, mandamus, prohibition and certiorari; and in cases involving personal freedom or the constitutionality of a law. It shall have appellate jurisdiction in criminal cases, where there has been a conviction for a felony or misdemeanor in a circuit court, and such appellate jurisdiction as may be conferred upon it by law where there has been such a conviction in any other court. In criminal proceedings relating to the public revenue, the right of appeal shall belong to the state as well as to the defendant. It shall have such other appellate jurisdiction, in both civil and criminal cases, as may be prescribed by law.

The court shall have power to promulgate rules for all cases and proceedings, civil and criminal, for all of the courts of the state relating to writs, warrants, process, practice and procedure, which shall have the force and effect of law.

The court shall have general supervisory control over all intermediate appellate courts, circuit courts and magistrate courts. The chief justice shall be the administrative head of all the courts. He may assign a judge from one intermediate appellate court to another, from one circuit court to another, or from one magistrate court to another, for temporary service. The court shall appoint an administrative director to serve at its pleasure at a salary to be fixed by the court. The administrative director shall, under the direction of the chief justice, prepare and submit a budget for the court.

The officers and employees of the supreme court of appeals, including the clerk and the law librarian, shall be appointed and may be removed by the court. Their duties and compensation shall be prescribed by the court.

The number, times and places of the terms of the supreme court of appeals shall be prescribed by law. There shall be at least two terms of the court held annually.

Section 4. Writ of Error, Supersedeas and Appeal; Scope and Form of Decisions

A writ of error, supersedeas or appeal shall be allowed by the supreme court of appeals, or a justice thereof, only upon a petition assigning error in the judgment or proceedings of a court and then only after the court, or a justice thereof, shall have examined and considered the record and is satisfied that there probably is error in the record, or that it presents a point proper for the consideration of the court.

No decision rendered by the court shall be considered as binding authority upon any court, except in the particular case decided, unless a majority of the justices of the court concur in such decision.

When a judgment or order of another court is reversed, modified or affirmed by the court, every point fairly arising upon the record shall be considered and decided; the reasons therefor shall be concisely stated in writing and preserved with the record; and it shall be the duty of the court to prepare a syllabus of the points adjudicated in each case in which an opinion is written and in which a majority of the justices thereof concurred, which shall be prefixed to the published report of the case.

Section 5. Circuit Courts

The judge or judges of each circuit court shall be elected by the voters of the circuit for a term of eight years, unless sooner removed or retired as authorized in this article. The Legislature may prescribe by law whether the election of such judges is to be on a partisan or nonpartisan basis. Upon the effective date of this article, each statutory court of record of limited jurisdiction existing in the state immediately prior to such effective date shall become part of the circuit court for the circuit in which it presently exists, and each such judge of such statutory court of record of limited jurisdiction shall thereupon become a judge of such circuit court. During his continuance in office, a judge of a circuit court shall reside in the circuit of which he is a judge.

The Legislature may increase, or other than during term of office decrease, the number of circuit judges within any circuit. The judicial circuits in existence on the effective date of this article shall remain as so constituted until changed by law, and the Legislature, at any session thereof held in the odd-numbered year next preceding the time for the full-term election of the judges thereof, may rearrange the circuits and may increase or diminish the number of circuits. A judge of a circuit court in office at the time of any such change shall continue as a judge of the circuit in which he shall continue to reside after such change until his term shall expire, unless sooner removed or retired as authorized in this article.

There shall be at least one judge for each circuit court and as many more as may be necessary to transact the business of such court. If there be two or more judges of a circuit court, provision shall be made by rules of such circuit court for the selection of one of such judges to serve as chief judge thereof. If the chief judge is temporarily disqualified or unable to serve, one of the judges of the circuit court designated in accordance with the rules of such court shall serve temporarily in his stead.

The supreme court of appeals shall provide for dividing the business of those circuits in which there shall be more than one judge between the judges thereof so as to promote and secure the convenient and expeditious transaction of such business.

In every county in the state the circuit court for such county shall sit at least three times in each year. The supreme court of appeals shall designate the times at which each circuit court shall sit, but until this action is taken by the supreme court of appeals, each circuit court shall sit at the times prescribed by law. If there be two or more judges of a circuit court, such judges may hold court in the same county or in different counties within the circuit at the same time or at different times.

Section 6. Circuit Court; Jurisdiction, Authority and Power

Circuit courts shall have control of all proceedings before magistrate courts by mandamus, prohibition and certiorari.

Circuit courts shall have original and general jurisdiction of all civil cases at law where the value or amount in controversy, exclusive of interest and costs, exceeds one hundred dollars unless such value or amount is increased by the Legislature; of all civil cases in equity; of proceedings in habeas corpus, mandamus, quo warranto, prohibition and certiorari; and of all crimes and misdemeanors. On and after January one, one thousand nine hundred seventy-six, the Legislature may provide that all matters of probate, the appointment and qualification of personal representatives, guardians, committees and curators, and the settlements of their accounts, shall be vested exclusively in circuit courts or their officers, but until such time as the Legislature provides otherwise, jurisdiction in such matters shall remain in the county commissions or tribunals existing in lieu thereof or the officers of such county commissions or tribunals.

Circuit courts shall have appellate jurisdiction in all cases, civil and criminal, where an appeal, writ of error or supersedeas is allowed by law to the judgment or proceedings of any magistrate court, unless such jurisdiction is conferred by law exclusively upon an intermediate appellate court or the supreme court of appeals.

Circuit courts shall also have such other jurisdiction, authority or power, original or appellate or concurrent, as may be prescribed by law.

Subject to the approval of the supreme court of appeals, each circuit court shall have the authority and power to establish local rules to govern the court.

Subject to the supervisory control of the supreme court of appeals, each circuit court shall have general supervisory control over all magistrate courts in the circuit. Under the direction of the chief justice of the supreme court of appeals, the judge of the circuit court, or the chief judge thereof if there be more than one judge of the circuit court, shall be the administrative head of the circuit court and all magistrate courts in the circuit.

Section 7. General Provisions Relating to Justices, Judges, and Magistrates

All justices, judges and magistrates must be residents of this state and shall be commissioned by the governor. No person may hereafter be elected as a justice of the supreme court of appeals unless he has been admitted to practice law for at least ten years prior to his election, and no person may hereafter be elected as a judge of a circuit court unless he has been admitted to practice law for at least five years prior to his election.

Justices, judges and magistrates shall receive the salaries fixed by law, which shall be paid entirely out of the state treasury, and which may be increased but shall not be diminished during their term of office, and they shall receive expenses as provided by law. The salary of a circuit judge shall also not be diminished during his term of office by virtue of the statutory courts of record of limited jurisdiction of his circuit becoming a part of such circuit as provided in section five of this article.

Any justice of the supreme court of appeals and any judge of any circuit court, including any statutory court of record of limited jurisdiction which becomes a part of a circuit court by virtue of section five of this article, in office on the effective date of this article shall continue in office until his term shall expire, unless sooner removed or retired as authorized in this article: Provided, That as to the term of any judge of a statutory court of record of limited jurisdiction which does not expire on the thirty-first day of December, one thousand nine hundred seventy-six, the following provisions shall govern and control unless any such judges shall be sooner removed or retired as authorized in this article:

(1) If the term would otherwise expire before the thirty-first day of December, one thousand nine hundred seventy-six, such term shall continue through and expire on said thirty-first day of December, one thousand nine hundred seventy-six.

(2) if the term would otherwise expire on the first day of January, one thousand nine hundred seventy-seven, such term shall terminate and expire on the thirty-first day of December, one thousand nine hundred seventy-six, and

(3) if the term would otherwise expire after the thirty-first day of December, one thousand nine hundred seventy-six, but other than on the first day of January, one thousand nine hundred seventy-seven, such term shall continue through and expire on the thirty-first day of December, one thousand nine hundred eighty-four.

No justice, judge or magistrate shall hold any other office, or accept any appointment or public trust, under this or any other government; nor shall he become a candidate for any elective public office or nomination thereto, except a judicial office; and the violation of any of these provisions shall vacate his judicial office. No justice of the supreme court of appeals or judge of an intermediate appellate court or of a circuit court shall practice the profession of law during the term of his office, but magistrates who are licensed to practice this profession may practice law except to the extent prohibited by the Legislature.

If from any cause a vacancy shall occur in the office of a justice of the supreme court of appeals or a judge of a circuit court, the governor shall issue a directive of election to fill such vacancy in the manner prescribed by law for electing a justice or judge of the court in which the vacancy exists, and the justice or judge shall be elected for the unexpired term; and in the meantime, the governor shall fill such vacancy by appointment until a justice or judge shall be elected and qualified. If the unexpired term be less than two years, or such additional period, not exceeding a total of three years, as may be prescribed by law, the governor shall fill such vacancy by appointment for the unexpired term.

Section 8. Censure, Temporary Suspension and Retirement of Justices, Judges and Magistrates; Removal

Under its inherent rule-making power, which is hereby declared, the supreme court of appeals shall, from time to time, prescribe, adopt, promulgate and amend rules prescribing a judicial code of ethics, and a code of regulations and standards of conduct and performances for justices, judges and magistrates, along with sanctions and penalties for any violation thereof, and the supreme court of appeals is authorized to censure or temporarily suspend any justice, judge or magistrate having the judicial power of the state, including one of its own members, for any violation of any such code of ethics, code of regulations and standards, or to retire any such justice, judge or magistrate who is eligible for retirement under the West Virginia judges' retirement system (or any successor or substituted retirement system for justices, judges and magistrates of this state) and who, because of advancing years and attendant physical or mental incapacity, should not, in the opinion of the supreme court of appeals, continue to serve as a justice, judge or magistrate.

No justice, judge or magistrate shall be censured, temporarily suspended or retired under the provisions of this section unless he shall have been afforded the right to have a hearing before the supreme court of appeals, nor unless he shall have received notice of the proceedings, with a statement of the cause or causes alleged for his censure, temporary suspension or retirement, at least twenty days before the day on which the proceeding is to commence. No justice of the supreme court of appeals may be temporarily suspended or retired unless all of the other justices concur in such temporary suspension or retirement. When rules herein authorized are prescribed, adopted and promulgated, they shall supersede all laws and parts of laws in conflict therewith, and such laws shall be and become of no further force or effect to the extent of such conflict.

A retired justice or judge may, with his permission and with the approval of the supreme court of appeals, be recalled by the chief justice of the supreme court of appeals for temporary assignment as a justice of the supreme court of appeals, or judge of an intermediate appellate court, a circuit court or a magistrate court.

A justice or judge may be removed only by impeachment in accordance with the provisions of section nine, article four of this constitution. A magistrate may be removed from office in the manner provided by law for the removal of county officers.

Section 9. Clerks of Circuit Courts

The voters of each county shall elect a clerk of the circuit court, whose term of office shall be six years; his duties, responsibilities, compensation and the manner of removing him from office shall be prescribed by law. Whenever the clerk shall be so situated as to make it improper for him to act in any matter, a clerk to act therein shall be appointed by the judge of the circuit court or the chief judge thereof, if there be more than one judge of the circuit court. Vacancies shall be filled in the manner prescribed by law. A clerk of the circuit court in office on the effective date of this article shall continue in office until his term shall expire, unless sooner removed in the manner prescribed by law.

Section 10. Magistrate Courts

The Legislature shall establish in each county a magistrate court or courts with the right of appeal as prescribed by law. Such courts shall be courts of record if so prescribed by law.

The Legislature shall determine the qualifications and the number of magistrates for each such court to be elected by the voters of the county, and the Legislature may prescribe by law whether the election of such magistrates is to be on a partisan or nonpartisan basis: Provided, That any person in office as a justice of the peace of this state on the effective date of this article and who has served as a justice of the peace of this state for at least one year prior to such effective date shall, insofar as any qualifications established by the Legislature for the office of magistrate are concerned and notwithstanding the same, be deemed qualified for life to run for election as a magistrate of any such court: And provided further, That the Legislature shall not have the power to require that a magistrate be a person licensed to practice the profession of law, nor shall any justice or judge of any higher court establish any rules which by their nature would dictate or mandate that a magistrate be a person licensed to practice the profession of law. The magistrates of such courts shall hold their offices for the term of four years unless sooner removed or retired as authorized in this article. The Legislature shall also determine the number of officers to be selected for each such court and the manner of their selection. During his continuance in office a magistrate or officer of such a court shall reside in the county for which he is elected or selected. The Legislature shall prescribe by law for the filling of any vacancy in the office of a magistrate or officer of such court. The jurisdiction of a magistrate court shall extend throughout the county for which it is established, shall be uniform for all counties of the state and shall be subject to such regulations as to venue of actions and the counties in which process may be executed or served on parties or witnesses as may be prescribed by law. The times and places for holding such courts shall be designated or determined in such manner as shall be prescribed by law. Magistrate courts shall have such original jurisdiction in criminal matters as may be prescribed by law, but no person shall be convicted or sentenced for a felony in such courts. In criminal cases, the procedure may be by information or warrant of arrest, without presentment or indictment by a grand jury. Such courts shall have original jurisdiction in all civil cases at law wherein the value or amount in controversy, exclusive of interest and costs, shall not exceed fifteen hundred dollars, unless such amount and value shall be increased by the Legislature, except such civil matters as may be excluded from their jurisdiction by law; and, to the extent provided by law, in proceedings involving real estate when the title thereto is not in controversy. No judgment of a magistrate in any proceeding involving real estate or any right pertaining thereto shall bar the title of any party or any remedy therefor.

The division of the business of a magistrate court in any county in which there shall be more than one magistrate of such court between the magistrates thereof so as to promote and secure the convenient and expeditious transaction of such business shall be determined in such manner or by such method as shall be prescribed by the judge of the circuit court of such county, or the chief judge thereof, if there be more than one judge of such circuit court.

In a trial by jury in a magistrate court, the jury shall consist of six jurors who are qualified as prescribed by law.

No magistrate or any officer of a magistrate court shall be compensated for his services on a fee basis or receive to his own use for his services any pecuniary compensation, reward or benefit other than the salary prescribed by law.

Section 11. Municipal Courts

The Legislature may provide for the establishment in incorporated cities, towns or villages of municipal, police or mayors' courts, and may also provide the manner of selection of the judges of such courts. Such courts shall have jurisdiction to enforce municipal ordinances, with the right of appeal as prescribed by law. Until otherwise provided by law, all such courts heretofore established shall remain and continue as now constituted, and with the same right of appeal, insofar as their jurisdiction to enforce municipal ordinances is concerned; but on and after January one, one thousand nine hundred seventy-seven, any other jurisdiction now exercised by such courts shall cease. No judge of a municipal, police or mayor's court or any officer thereof shall be compensated for his services on a fee basis or receive to his own use for his services any pecuniary compensation, reward or benefit other than the salary prescribed therefor.

Section 12. Issuance and Execution of Writs, Warrants and Process; Admission to Bail

The Legislature may designate the courts and officers or deputies thereof who shall have the power to issue, execute or serve such writs, warrants or any other process as may be prescribed by law, and may specify before what courts or officers thereof such writs, warrants or other process shall be returnable. The Legislature may also designate the courts and officers or deputies thereof who shall have the power to admit persons to bail. No person exercising such powers shall be compensated therefor on a fee basis.

Section 13. Parts of Existing Law Effective

Except as otherwise provided in this article, such parts of the common law, and of the laws of this state as are in force on the effective date of this article and are not repugnant thereto, shall be and continue the law of this state until altered or repealed by the Legislature.

Section 14. Pending Causes; Transfer of Causes; Records

Until otherwise provided by law, all matters pending in any court on the effective date of this article shall remain and be prosecuted in the court in which they are pending.

Whenever the jurisciction, powers or duties of any court are terminated or changed, the Legislature shall provice by law for the transfer of all matters pending therein as to which the court shall not thereafter act, together with all of the records and papers pertaining thereto, to a court having jurisdiction, powers or duties as to such matters, and shall provide for the prosecution therein of such matters as if then and there pending.

All records and papers pertaining to matters already disposed of in any court shall be preserved or disposed of in a manner prescribed by law.

Section 15. Offices Phased Out; Effective Date of Article; Certain Provisions to be Operable at Time Specified; Effect of Article on Certain Provisions of Constitution

Notwithstanding the provisions of section one of this article, the office of justice of the peace, as heretofore constituted, shall continue until January one, one thousand nine hundred seventy-seven. No person shall be elected to the office of justice of the peace or constable at the general election to be held in the year one thousand nine hundred seventy-six, and said offices shall cease to exist as of January one, one thousand nine hundred seventy-seven.

This article shall take effect from the time of ratification, but in any case where it is specified in this article that a provision shall become operable on and after a certain date, such date shall govern and control as to the operable date of such provision.

The provisions of this article shall supersede and prevail over all other provisions of this constitution which are expressly or impliedly in conflict or inconsistent therewith.

Section 16. Family Courts

There is hereby created under the general supervisory control of the supreme court of appeals a unified family court system in the state of West Virginia to rule on family law and related matters. Family courts shall have original jurisdiction in the areas of family law and related matters as may hereafter be established by law. Family courts may also have such further jurisdiction as established by law.

Family court judges shall be elected by the voters for a term prescribed by law not to exceed eight years, unless sooner removed or retired as authorized in this article. Family court judges must be admitted to practice law in this state for at least five years prior to their election. Family court judges shall reside in the circuit for which he or she is a judge.

The necessary number of family court judges, the number of family court circuits and the arrangement of circuits shall be established by law. Staggered terms of office for family court judges may also be established by law.

The supreme court of appeals shall have general supervisory control over all family courts and may provide for the assignment of a family court judge to another court for temporary service. The provisions of section seven and eight of this article applicable to circuit judges shall also apply to family court judges.

ARTICLE IX: COUNTY ORGANIZATION

Section 1. County Organization

The voters of each county shall elect a surveyor of lands, a prosecuting attorney, a sheriff, and one and not more than two assessors, who shall hold their respective offices for the term of four years.

Section 2. Constables, coroners and overseers of the poor. There shall also be elected in each district of the county, by the voters thereof, one constable, and if the population of any district shall exceed twelve hundred, an additional constable, whose term of office shall be four years, and whose powers as such shall extend throughout their county. The assessor shall, with the advice and consent of the county court, have the power to appoint one or more assistants. Coroners, overseers of the poor and surveyors of roads, shall be appointed by the county court. The foregoing officers, except the prosecuting attorneys, shall reside in the county and district for which they shall be respectively elected.

Section 3. Sheriffs

A person who has been elected or who has served as sheriff during all or any part of two consecutive terms shall be ineligible for the office of sheriff during any part of the term immediately following the second of the two consecutive terms. The person holding the office of sheriff when this section is ratified shall not be prevented from holding the office of sheriff during the term immediately following the term he is then serving.

Section 4. Malfeasance and Misfeasance in Office

The presidents of the county courts, the justices of the peace, sheriffs, prosecuting attorneys, clerks of the circuit and of the county courts, and all other county officers shall be subject to indictment for malfeasance, misfeasance, or neglect of official duty and upon conviction thereof, their office shall become vacant.

Section 5. Commissioning of Officers not Otherwise Provided For

The Legislature shall provide for commissioning such of the officers herein mentioned, as it may deem proper, not provided for in this constitution, and may require any class of them to give bond with security for the faithful discharge of the duties of their respective offices.

Section 6. Compensation/Deputies

It shall further provide for the compensation, the duties and responsibilities of such officers, and may provide for the appointment of their deputies and assistants by general laws.

Section 7. Conservators of the Peace

The president of the county court and every justice and constable shall be a conservator of the peace throughout his county.

Section 8. Formation of New Counties

No new county shall hereafter be formed in this state with an area of less than four hundred square miles; nor with a population of less than six thousand; nor shall any county, from which a new county, or part thereof shall be taken, be reduced in area below four hundred square miles, nor in population below six thousand. Nor shall a new county be formed without the consent of a majority of the voters residing within the boundaries of the proposed new county, and voting on the question.

Section 9. County Commissions

The office of county court or tribunal in lieu thereof heretofore created is hereby continued in all respects as heretofore constituted, but from and after the effective date of this amendment shall be designated as the county commission and wherever in this constitution, the code of West Virginia, acts of the Legislature or elsewhere in law a reference is made to the county court of any county, such reference shall be read, construed and understood to mean the county commission.

Except as otherwise provided in section eleven or thirteen of this article, there shall be in each county of the state a county commission, composed of three commissioners, and two of said commissioners shall be a quorum for the transaction of business. It shall hold four regular sessions in each year, and at such times as may be fixed and entered of record by the said commission. Provisions may be made by law for holding special sessions of said commissions.

Section 10. Terms of Office of County Commissioners

The commissioners shall be elected by the voters of the county, and hold their office for a term of six years, except that at the first meeting of said commissioners they shall designate by lot, or otherwise in such manner as they may determine, one of their number, who shall hold his office for a term of two years, one for four years, and one for six years, so that one shall be elected every two years; but no two of said commissioners shall be elected from the same magisterial district. If two or more persons residing in the same district shall receive the greater number of votes cast at any election, then only the one of such persons receiving the highest number shall be declared elected, and the person living in another district, who shall receive the next highest number of votes, shall be declared elected. Said commissioners shall annually elect one of their number as president. The commissioners of said commissions, now in office, shall remain therein for the term for which they have been elected, unless sooner removed therefrom, in the manner prescribed by law.

Section 11. Powers of County Commissions

The county commissions, through their clerks, shall have the custody of all deeds and other papers presented for record in their counties, and the same shall be preserved therein, or otherwise disposed of, as now is, or may be prescribed by law. They shall also, under such regulations as may be prescribed by law, have the superintendence and administration of the internal police and fiscal affairs of their counties, including the establishment and regulation of roads, ways, bridges, public landings, ferries and mills, with authority to lay and disburse the county levies: Provided, That no license for the sale of intoxicating liquors in any incorporated city, town or village, shall be granted without the consent of the municipal authorities thereof, first had and obtained. Until otherwise prescribed by law, they shall, in all cases of contest, be the judge of the election, qualification and returns of their own members, and of all county and district officers, subject to such regulations, by appeal or otherwise, as may be prescribed by law. Such commissions may exercise such other powers, and perform such other duties, not of a judicial nature, as may be prescribed by law. Such existing tribunals as have been heretofore established by the Legislature to act as to police and fiscal matters in lieu of county commissions in certain counties shall remain and continue as now constituted in the counties in which they have been respectively established until otherwise provided by law, and they shall have and exercise the powers which the county commissions have under this article, and, until otherwise provided by law, such clerk as is mentioned in section twelve of this article shall exercise any powers and discharge any duties, heretofore conferred on, or required of, any such tribunal or the clerk of such tribunal respecting the recording and preservation of deeds and other papers presented for record and such other matters as are prescribed by law to be exercised and discharged by the clerk thereof.

Section 12. Clerk of County Commission

The voters of each county shall elect a clerk of the county commission, whose term of office shall be six years. His duties and compensation and the manner of his removal shall be prescribed by law. But the clerks of said commissions, now in office, shall remain therein for the term for which they have been elected, unless sooner removed therefrom, in the manner prescribed by law.

Section 13. Reformation of County Commissions

The Legislature shall, upon the application of any county, reform, alter or modify the county commission established by this article in such county, and in lieu thereof, with the assent of a majority of the voters of such county voting at an election, create another tribunal for the transaction of the business required to be performed by the county commission created by this article. Whenever a county commission shall receive a petition signed by ten percent of the registered voters of such county requesting the reformation, alteration or modification of such county commission, it shall be the mandatory duty of such county commission to request the Legislature, at its next regular session thereafter, to enact an act reforming, altering or modifying such county commission and establishing in lieu thereof another tribunal for the transaction of the business required to be performed by such county commission, such act to take effect upon the assent of the voters of such county, as aforesaid. Whenever any such tribunal is established, all of the provisions of this article in relation to the county commission shall be applicable to the tribunal established in lieu of said commission. When such tribunal has been established, it shall continue to act in lieu of the county commission until otherwise provided by law.

ARTICLE X: TAXATION AND FINANCE

Section 1. Taxation and Finance

Subject to the exceptions in this section contained, taxation shall be equal and uniform throughout the state, and all property, both real and personal, shall be taxed in proportion to its value to be ascertained as directed by law. No one species of property from which a tax may be collected shall be taxed higher than any other species of property of equal value; except that the aggregate of taxes assessed in any one year upon personal property employed exclusively in agriculture, including horticulture and grazing, products of agriculture as above defined, including livestock, while owned by the producer, and money, notes, bonds, bills and accounts receivable, stocks and other similar intangible personal property shall not exceed fifty cents on each one hundred dollars of value thereon and upon all property owned, used and occupied by the owner thereof exclusively for residential purposes and upon farms occupied and cultivated by their owners or bona fide tenants, one dollar; and upon all other property situated outside of municipalities, one dollar and fifty cents; and upon all other property situated within municipalities, two dollars; and the Legislature shall further provide by general law for increasing the maximum rates, authorized to be fixed, by the different levying bodies upon all classes of property, by submitting the question to the voters of the taxing units affected, but no increase shall be effective unless at least sixty percent of the qualified voters shall favor such increase, and such increase shall not continue for a longer period than three years at any one time, and shall never exceed by more than fifty percent the maximum rate herein provided and prescribed by law; and the revenue derived from this source shall be apportioned by the Legislature among the levying units of the state in proportion to the levy laid in said units upon real and other personal property; but property used for educational, literary, scientific, religious or charitable purposes, all cemeteries, public property, the personal property, including livestock, employed exclusively in agriculture as above defined and the products of agriculture as so defined while owned by the producers may by law be exempted from taxation; household goods to the value of two hundred dollars shall be exempted from taxation. The Legislature shall have authority to tax privileges, franchises, and incomes of persons and corporations and to classify and graduate the tax on all incomes according to the amount thereof and to exempt from taxation incomes below a minimum to be fixed from time to time, and such revenues as may be derived from such tax may be appropriated as the Legislature may provide. After the year nineteen hundred thirty-three, the rate of the state tax upon property shall not exceed one cent upon the hundred dollars valuation, except to pay the principal and interest of bonded indebtedness of the state now existing.

Section 1a. Exemptions From and Additional Adjustments to Ad Valorem Property Taxation

Notwithstanding the provisions of sections one and one-b of this article, household goods and personal effects, if such household goods or personal effects are not held or used for profit, and all intangible personal property shall be exempt from ad valorem property taxation: Provided, That intangible personal property may be made subject to such taxation only to the extent provided by the Legislature by general law not inconsistent with this section.

The Legislature shall not impose ad valorem property taxation upon money, bank deposits and other investments determined by such law to be in the nature of deposits in a bank or other financial institution, or upon pensions, moneys or investments determined by the Legislature in such law to be in lieu of or otherwise in the nature of pensions.

The Legislature by general law may exempt from such taxation any amount of the value of all or certain intangible personal property and any type, group or class of such intangibles but such exemptions shall be uniform throughout the state. No tax imposed upon such intangibles shall be at a rate or rates in excess of the maximum rate permitted to be imposed upon personal property employed exclusively in agriculture as provided in sections one, one-b or ten of this article, as the case may be, in the county wherein the intangible personal property has situs, as such situs is determined by the Legislature in such general law.

The valuations with respect to property acquired or created subsequent to any statewide reappraisal and the valuations with respect to any intangible personal property subjected to ad valorem property taxation pursuant to this section shall be allocated and phased-in over a period of years and be valued with respect to the same base year as other property subject to ad valorem property taxation in order to provide for equitable and similar treatment of such property subsequently acquired or created or such intangible personal property as compared to similarly situated previously existing property of similar value whose owner is receiving the benefit of any allocation and phase-in allowed pursuant to section one-b of this article.

Any intangible personal property which would be subject to ad valorem property taxation under prior provisions of this Constitution shall continue to be subjected to such taxation as provided by and in accordance with current statutory law for the assessment of such taxes upon such property, which laws are hereby validated for such purpose or purposes, until the first day of July in the year one thousand nine hundred eighty-five or until the first statewide reappraisal of property pursuant to section one-b of this article shall be first implemented and employed to fix values for ad valorem property taxation, whichever shall last occur, and thereafter no intangible personal property shall be subject to such taxation save for and except as provided by the Legislature by general law enacted after the ratification of the amendment of this section in the year one thousand nine hundred eighty-four.

Section 1b. Property Tax Limitation and Homestead Exemption Amendment of 1982

Ad valorem property taxation shall be in accordance with this section and other applicable provisions of this article not inconsistent with this section.

> Subsection A -- Value; Rate of Assessment; Exceptions

Notwithstanding any other provisions of this Constitution and except as otherwise provided in this section, all property subject to ad valorem taxation shall be assessed at sixty percent of its value, as directed to be ascertained in this section, except that the Legislature may from time to time, by general law agreed to by two thirds of the members elected to each house, establish a higher percentage for the purposes of this paragraph, which percentage shall be uniform as to all classes of property defined in section one of this article, but not more than one hundred percent of such value.

Notwithstanding the foregoing, for the first day of July, one thousand nine hundred eighty-two, and the first day of July of each year thereafter until the values may be fixed as a result of the first statewide reappraisal hereinafter required, assessments shall be made under the provisions of current statutory law, which is hereby validated for such purpose until and unless amended by the Legislature. Assessment and taxation in accord with this section shall be deemed to be equal and uniform for all purposes.

> Subsection B -- Determination of Value

The Legislature shall provide by general law for periodic statewide reappraisal of all property, which reappraisal shall be related for all property to a specified base year which, as to each such reappraisal, shall be uniform for each appraisal for all classes of property and all counties. In such law, the Legislature shall provide for consideration of:

(1) trends in market values over a fixed period of years prior to the base year,

(2) the location of the property, and

(3) such other factors and methods as it may determine: Provided, That with respect to reappraisal of all property upon the base year of one thousand nine hundred eighty, such reappraisals are deemed to be valid and in compliance with this section: Provided, however, That with respect to farm property, as defined from time to time by the Legislature by general law, the determination of value shall be according to its fair and reasonable value for farming purposes, as may be defined by general law.

The results of each statewide appraisal shall upon completion be certified and published and errors therein may be corrected, all as provided by general law. The first such statewide appraisal shall be completed, certified and published on or before the thirty-first day of March, one thousand nine hundred eighty-five, for use when directed by the Legislature.

The Legislature shall further prescribe by general law the manner in which each statewide reappraisal shall be employed to establish the value of the various separately assessed parcels or interests in parcels of real property and various items of personal property subject to ad valorem property taxation, the methods by which increases and reductions in value subsequent to the base year of each statewide reappraisal shall be ascertained, and require the enforcement thereof.

Subsection C -- General Homestead Exemption

Notwithstanding any other provisions of this Constitution to the contrary, the first twenty thousand dollars of assessed valuation of any real property, or of personal property in the form of a mobile home, used exclusively for residential purposes and occupied by the owner or one of the owners thereof as his residence who is a citizen of this state and who is sixty-five years of age or older or is permanently and totally disabled as that term may be defined by the Legislature, shall be exempt from ad valorem property taxation, subject to such requirements, limitations and conditions as shall be prescribed by general law.

Notwithstanding any other provision of this Constitution to the contrary, the Legislature shall have the authority to provide by general law for an exemption from ad valorem property taxation in an amount not to exceed the first twenty thousand dollars of value of any real property, or of personal property in the form of a mobile home, used exclusively for residential purposes and occupied by the owner or one of the owners thereof as his residence who is a citizen of this state, and who is under sixty-five years of age and not totally and permanently disabled: Provided, That upon enactment of such general law, this exemption shall only apply to such property in any county in which the property was appraised at its value as of the first day of January, one thousand nine hundred eighty, or thereafter, as determined by the Legislature, and this exemption shall be phased in over such period of time not to exceed five years from the date such property was so appraised, or such longer time as the Legislature may determine by general law: Provided, however, That in no event shall any one person and his spouse, or one homestead be entitled to more than one exemption under these provisions: Provided further, That these provisions are subject to such requirements, limitations and conditions as shall be prescribed by general law.

The Legislature shall have the authority to provide by general law for property tax relief to citizens of this state who are tenants of residential or farm property.

Subsection D -- Additional Limitations on Value

With respect to the first statewide reappraisal, pursuant to this section, the resulting increase in value in each and every parcel of land or interest therein and various items of personal property subject to ad valorem property taxation over and above the previously assessed value shall be allocated over a period of ten years in equal amounts annually.

The Legislature may by general law also provide for the phasing in of any subsequent statewide reappraisal of property.

Subsection E -- Levies for Free Schools

In equalizing the support of free schools provided by state and local taxes, the Legislature may require that the local school districts levy all or any portion of the maximum levies allowed under section one of this article which has been allocated to such local school districts.

Within the limits of the maximum levies permitted for excess levies for schools or better schools in sections one and ten of this article, the Legislature may, in lieu of the exercise of such powers by the local school districts as heretofore provided, submit to the voters, by general law, a statewide excess levy, and if it be approved by the required number of voters, impose such levy, subject however to all the limitations and requirements for the approval of such levies as in the case of a district levy. The law submitting the question to the voters shall provide, upon approval of the levy by the voters, for the assumption of the obligation of any local excess levies for schools then in force theretofore authorized by the voters of a local taxing unit to the extent of such excess levies imposed by the state and so as to avoid double taxation of those local districts. The Legislature may also by general law reserve to the school districts such portions of the power to lay authorized excess levies as it may deem appropriate to enable local school districts to provide educational services which are not required to be furnished or supported by the state. If a statewide excess levy for the support of free schools is approved by the required majority, the revenue from such a statewide excess levy shall be deposited in the state treasury and be allocated first for the local obligations assumed and thereafter for such part of the state effort to support free schools, by appropriation or as the law submitting the levy to the voters shall require, as the case may be.

The defeat of any such proposed statewide excess levy for school purposes shall not in any way abrogate or impair any local existing excess levy for such purpose nor prevent the adoption of any future local excess levy for such purpose.

Subsection F -- Implementation

In the event of any inconsistency between any of the provisions of this section and other provisions of this Constitution, the provisions of this section shall prevail. The Legislature shall have plenary power to provide by general law for the equitable application of this article and, as to taxes to be assessed prior to the first statewide reappraisal, to make such laws retroactive to the first day of July, one thousand nine hundred eighty-two, or thereafter.

Section 1c. Exemption From Ad Valorem Taxation of Certain Personal Property of Inventory and Warehouse Goods, With Phase in to Full Exemption Over Five-Year Period

Notwithstanding any other provisions of this Constitution, tangible personal property which is moving in interstate commerce through or over the territory of the State of West Virginia, or which was consigned from a point of origin outside the State to a warehouse, public or private, within the State for storage in transit to a final destination outside the State, whether specified when transportation begins or afterward, but in any case specified timely for exempt status determination purposes, shall not be deemed to have acquired a tax situs in West Virginia for purposes of ad valorem taxation and shall be exempt from such taxation, except as otherwise provided in this section. Such property shall not be deprived of such exemption because while in the warehouse the personal property is assembled, bound, joined, processed, disassembled, divided, cut, broken in bulk, relabeled, or repackaged for delivery out of state, unless such activity results in a new or different product, article, substance or commodity, or one of different utility. Personal property of inventories of natural resources shall not be exempt from ad valorem taxation unless required by paramount federal law.

The exemption allowed by the preceding paragraph shall be phased in over a period of five consecutive assessment years, at the rate of one fifth of the assessed value of the property per assessment year, beginning the first day of July, one thousand nine hundred eighty-seven.

Section 2.

Repealed

Section 3. Receipts and Expenditures of Public Moneys

No money shall be drawn from the treasury but in pursuance of an appropriation made by law, and on a warrant issued thereon by the auditor; nor shall any money or fund be taken for any other purpose than that for which it has been or may be appropriated or provided. A complete and detailed statement of the receipts and expenditures of the public moneys shall be published annually.

Section 4. Limitation on Contracting of State Debt

No debt shall be contracted by this state, except to meet casual deficits in the revenue, to redeem a previous liability of the state, to suppress insurrection, repel invasion or defend the state in time of war; but the payment of any liability other than that for the ordinary expenses of the state, shall be equally distributed over a period of at least twenty years.

Section 5. Power of Taxation

The power of taxation of the Legislature shall extend to provisions for the payment of the state debt, and interest thereon, the support of free schools, and the payment of the annual estimated expenses of the state; but whenever any deficiency in the revenue shall exist in any year, it shall, at the regular session thereof held next after the deficiency occurs, levy a tax for the ensuing year, sufficient with the other sources of income, to meet such deficiency, as well as the estimated expenses of such year.

Section 6. Credit of State not to be Granted in Certain Cases

The credit of the state shall not be granted to, or in aid of any county, city, township, corporation or person; nor shall the state ever assume, or become responsible for the debts or liabilities of any county, city, township, corporation or person. The investment of state or public funds shall be subject to procedures and guidelines heretofore or hereafter established by the Legislature for the prudent investment of such funds.
Section 6a. Appropriations and taxation for the benefit of counties, municipalities or other political subdivisions of the state.

Notwithstanding the provisions of section six of this article,

(1) the Legislature may appropriate state funds for use in matching or maximizing grants-in-aid for public purposes from the United States or any department, bureau, commission or agency thereof, or any other source, to any county, municipality or other political subdivision of the state, under such circumstances and subject to such terms, conditions and restrictions as the Legislature may prescribe by law, and

(2) the Legislature may impose a state tax or taxes or dedicate a state tax or taxes or any portion thereof for the benefit of and use by counties, municipalities or other political subdivisions of the state for public purposes, the proceeds of any such imposed or dedicated tax or taxes or portion thereof to be distributed to such counties, municipalities or other political subdivisions of the state under such circumstances and subject to such terms, conditions and restrictions as the Legislature may prescribe by law.

Section 7. Duties of County Authorities in Assessing Taxes

County authorities shall never assess taxes, in any one year, the aggregate of which shall exceed ninety-five cents per one hundred dollars' valuation, except for the support of free schools; payment of indebtedness existing at the time of the adoption of this constitution; and for the payment of any indebtedness with the interest thereon, created under the succeeding section, unless such assessment, with all questions involving the increase of such aggregate, shall have been submitted to the vote of the people of the county, and have received three fifths of all the votes cast for and against it.

Section 8. Bonded Indebtedness of Counties, Etc.

No county, city, school district, or municipal corporation, except in cases where such corporations have already authorized their bonds to be issued, shall hereafter be allowed to become indebted, in any manner, or for any purpose, to an amount, including existing indebtedness, in the aggregate, exceeding five per centum on the value of the taxable property therein to be ascertained by the last assessment for state and county taxes, previous to the incurring of such indebtedness; nor without, at the same time, providing for the collection of a direct annual tax on all taxable property therein, in the ratio, as between the several classes or types of such taxable property, specified in section one of this article, separate and apart from and in addition to all other taxes for all other purposes, sufficient to pay, annually, the interest on such debt, and the principal thereof, within, and not exceeding thirty-four years. Such tax, in an amount sufficient to pay the interest and principal on bonds issued by any school district not exceeding in the aggregate three per centum of such assessed value, may be levied outside the limits fixed by section one of this article: Provided, That no debt shall be contracted under this section, unless all questions connected with the same, shall have been first submitted to a vote of the people, and have received three fifths of all the votes cast for and against the same.

Section 8a. Issuance of bonds or other obligations payable from property taxes on increases in value due to economic development or redevelopment projects in counties and municipalities.

Notwithstanding any other provision of this Constitution to the contrary, the Legislature by general law may authorize the issuance of revenue bonds or other obligations by counties and municipalities to assist in financing qualified economic development or redevelopment projects that benefit public health, welfare and safety subject to conditions, restrictions or limitations as the Legislature may prescribe by general law.

The bonds or other obligations are payable from property tax revenues generated by the increases in value of property located within the development or redevelopment project area or district due to capital investment in the project. The Legislature shall prescribe by general law the manner in which these increases are determined.

The term for any bonds or other obligations issued may not exceed thirty tax years. The bonds or other obligations may not be deemed to be general obligations of the issuing county or municipality or of this state. The bonds or other obligations may provide for the pledge of any other funds as the owner of the improvements may by contract or otherwise be required to pay. Upon payment in full of the bonds, the increased tax revenues shall revert to the levying bodies authorized under the provisions of this Constitution to receive the revenues. The bonds or other obligations may not be paid from excess levy, bond levy or other special levy revenues.

Section 9. Municipal Taxes to be Uniform

The Legislature may, by law, authorize the corporate authorities of cities, towns and villages, for corporate purposes, to assess and collect taxes; but such taxes shall be uniform, with respect to persons and property within the jurisdiction of the authority imposing the same.

Section 10. School Levy and Bond Amendment.

Notwithstanding any other provision of the Constitution to the contrary, the maximum rates authorized and allocated by law for tax levies on the several classes of property for the support of public schools may be increased in any school district for a period not to exceed five years, and in an amount not to exceed one hundred percent of such maximum rates, if such increase is approved, in the manner provided by law, by at least a majority of the votes cast for and against the same.

Notwithstanding any other provision of the Constitution to the contrary, the maximum rates provided for tax levies by school districts on the several classes of property may be used entirely for current expense purposes; and all levies required for principal and interest payments on any bonded indebtedness, now or hereafter contracted, not to exceed five per cent on the value of the taxable property therein, the value to be ascertained in accordance with section eight of this article, shall be laid separate and apart and in addition to such maximum rates, but in the same proportions as such maximum rates are levied on the several classes of property.

Notwithstanding the provisions of section eight of this article relating to a vote of the people or any other provisions of this Constitution, a county board of education may contract indebtedness and issue bonds for public school purposes as provided by law, if, when submitted to a vote of the people of the county, in the manner provided by law, the question of contracting indebtedness and issuing bonds is approved by a majority of the votes cast for and against the same

Section 11. County and Municipal Excess Levy Amendment

Notwithstanding any other provision of this Constitution to the contrary, the maximum rates authorized and allocated by law for tax levies on the several classes of property by county commissions and municipalities may be increased in any county or municipality, as provided in section one of this article, for a period not to exceed five years.

Resolved further, That in accordance with the provisions of article eleven, chapter three of the code of West Virginia, one thousand nine hundred thirty-one, as amended, such proposed amendment is hereby numbered "Amendment No. 2" and designated as the "Equalizing Number of Years of Excess Levies Amendment" and the purpose of the proposed amendment is summarized as follows: "The purpose of this amendment is to allow county and municipal governments to propose excess levies for the same time periods as boards of education, which is up to five years."

Section 12. Nonprofit Youth Organization Revenue Exemption

Notwithstanding any provision of this Constitution to the contrary, real property in this state which is owned by a non-profit organization that has as its primary purpose the development of youth through adventure, educational or recreational activities for young people and others, which property contains facilities built at a cost of not less than $100,000,000 and which property is capable of supporting additional activities within the region and the State of West Virginia is exempt from ad valorem property taxation whether or not such property is used for the nonprofit organization's nonprofit purpose to generate revenue for the benefit of the non-profit organization subject to any requirements, limtations and conditions as may be prescribed by general law: Provided, That the tax exemption authorized by the provisions of this section shall not become effective until the Legislature adopts enabling legislation authorizing the exemption's implementation and concurrently prescribing requirements, limitations and conditions for the use of the tax exempt facility that protect local and regionally located businesses from use of the tax exempt facility in a manner that causes unfair competition and unreasonable loss of revenue to those businesses.

ARTICLE XI: CORPORATIONS

Section 1. Corporations

The Legislature shall provide for the organization of all corporations hereafter to be created, by general laws, uniform as to the class to which they relate; but no corporation shall be created by special law: Provided, That nothing in this section contained, shall prevent the Legislature from providing by special laws for the connection, by canal, of the waters of the Chesapeake with the Ohio River by line of the James River, Greenbrier, New River and Great Kanawha.

Section 2. Corporate Liability for Indebtedness

The stockholders of all corporations and joint-stock companies, except banks and banking institutions, created by laws of this state, shall be liable for the indebtedness of such corporations to the amount of their stock subscribed and unpaid, and no more.

Section 3. Exclusive Privileges Prohibited

All existing charters or grants of special or exclusive privileges under which organization shall not have taken place, or which shall not have been in operation within two years from the time this constitution takes effect, shall thereafter have no validity or effect whatever: Provided, That nothing herein shall prevent the execution of any bona fide contract heretofore lawfully made in relation to any existing charter or grant in this state.

Section 4. Rights of Stockholders

The Legislature shall provide by law that every corporation, other than a banking institution, shall have power to issue one or more classes and series within classes of stock, with or without par value, with full, limited or no voting powers, and with preferences and special rights and qualifications, and that in all elections for directors or managers of incorporated companies, every stockholder holding stock having the right to vote for directors, shall have the right to vote, in person or by proxy, for the number of shares of stock owned by him, for as many persons as there are directors or managers to be elected, or to cumulate said shares, and give one candidate as many votes as the number of directors multiplied by the number of his shares of stock shall equal, or to distribute them on the same principle among as many candidates as he shall think fit; and such directors or managers shall not be elected in any other manner.

Section 5. Street Railroads

No law shall be passed by the Legislature, granting the right to construct and operate a street railroad within any city, town or incorporated village, without requiring the consent of the local authorities having the control of the street or highway proposed to be occupied by such street railroad.

Section 6. Banks

The Legislature may provide by general law for the creation, organization, and regulation of banking institutions.

Section 7. Railroads

Every railroad corporation organized or doing business in this state shall annually, by their proper officers, make a report under oath, to the auditor of public accounts of this state, or some officer to be designated by law, setting forth the condition of their affairs, the operations of the year, and such other matters relating to their respective railroads as may be prescribed by law. The Legislature shall pass laws enforcing by suitable penalties the provisions of this section.

Section 8. Rolling Stock Considered Personal Property

The rolling stock and all other movable property belonging to any railroad company or corporation in this state, shall be considered personal property and shall be liable to execution and sale in the same manner as the personal property of individuals; and the Legislature shall pass no law exempting any such property from execution and sale.

Section 9. Railroads Public Highways

Railroads heretofore constructed, or that may hereafter be constructed in this state, are hereby declared public highways and shall be free to all persons for the transportation of their persons and property thereon, under such regulations as shall be prescribed by law; and the Legislature shall, from time to time, pass laws, applicable to all railroad corporations in the state, establishing reasonable maximum rates of charges for the transportation of passengers and freights, and providing for the correction of abuses, the prevention of unjust discriminations between through and local or way freight and passenger tariffs, and for the protection of the just rights of the public, and shall enforce such laws by adequate penalties.

Section 10. Stations to be Established

The Legislature shall, in the law regulating railway companies, require railroads running through, or within a half mile of a town or village, containing three hundred or more inhabitants, to establish stations for the accommodation of trade and travel of said town or village.

Section 11. Competing Lines/Legislative Permission

No railroad corporation shall consolidate its stock, property or franchise with any other railroad owning a parallel or competing line, or obtain the possession or control of such parallel or competing line, by lease or other contract, without the permission of the Legislature.

Section 12. Right of Eminent Domain

The exercise of the power and the right of eminent domain shall never be so construed or abridged as to prevent the taking, by the Legislature, of the property and franchises of incorporated companies already organized, and subjecting them to the public use, the same as of individuals.

ARTICLE XII: EDUCATION

Section 1. Education

The Legislature shall provide, by general law, for a thorough and efficient system of free schools.

Section 2. Supervision of Free Schools

The general supervision of the free schools of the State shall be vested in the West Virginia board of education which shall perform such duties as may be prescribed by law. The board shall consist of nine members to be appointed by the governor, by and with the advice and consent of the senate, for overlapping terms of nine years, except that the original appointments shall be for terms of one, two, three, four, five, six, seven, eight, and nine years, respectively. No more than five members of the board shall belong to the same political party, and in addition to the general qualifications otherwise required by the Constitution, the legislature may require other specific qualifications for membership on the board. No member of the board may be removed from office by the governor except for official misconduct, incompetence, neglect of duty, or gross immorality, and then only in the manner prescribed by law for the removal by the governor of state elective officers.

The West Virginia board of education shall in the manner prescribed by law, select the state superintendent of free schools who shall serve at its will and pleasure. He shall be the chief school officer of the State and shall have such powers and shall perform such duties as may be prescribed by law.

The state superintendent of free schools shall be a member of the board of public works as provided by subsection B, section fifty-one, article six of this Constitution.

Section 3. County Superintendents

The Legislature may provide for county superintendents and such other officers as may be necessary to carry out the objects of this article and define their duties, powers and compensation.

Section 4. Existing Permanent and Invested School Fund

The existing permanent and invested school fund, and all money accruing to this state from forfeited, delinquent, waste and unappropriated lands; and from lands heretofore sold for taxes and purchased by the state of Virginia, if hereafter redeemed or sold to others than this state; all grants, devises or bequests that may be made to this state, for the purposes of education or where the purposes of such grants, devises or bequests are not specified; this state's just share of the literary fund of Virginia, whether paid over or otherwise liquidated; and any sums of money, stocks or property which this state shall have the right to claim from the state of Virginia for educational purposes; the proceeds of the estates of persons who may die without leaving a will or heir, and of all escheated lands; the proceeds of any taxes that may be levied on the revenues of any corporations; all moneys that may be paid as an equivalent for exemption from military duty; and such sums as may from time to time be appropriated by the Legislature for the purpose, shall be set apart as a separate fund to be called the "School Fund," and invested under such regulations as may be prescribed by law, in the interest-bearing securities of the United States, or of this state, or if such interest-bearing securities cannot be obtained, then said "School Fund" shall be invested in such other solvent, interest-bearing securities as shall be approved by the governor, superintendent of free schools, auditor and treasurer, who are hereby constituted the "Board of the School Fund," to manage the same under such regulations as may be prescribed by law; and the interest thereof shall be annually applied to the support of free schools throughout the state, and to no other purpose whatever. But any portion of said interest remaining unexpended at the close of a fiscal year shall be added to and remain a part of the capital of the "School Fund": Provided, That all taxes which shall be received by the state upon delinquent lands, except the taxes due to the state thereon, shall be refunded to the county or district by or for which the same were levied.

Section 5. Support of Free Schools

The Legislature shall provide for the support of free schools by appropriating thereto the interest of the invested "School Fund," the net proceeds of all forfeitures and fines accruing to this state under the laws thereof and by general taxation of persons and property or otherwise. It shall also provide for raising in each county or district, by the authority of the people thereof, such a proportion of the amount required for the support of free schools therein as shall be prescribed by general laws.

Section 6. School Districts

The school districts into which the state is divided shall continue until changed pursuant to act of the Legislature: Provided, That the school board of any district shall be elected by the voters of the respective district without reference to political party affiliation. No more than two of the members of such board may be residents of the same magisterial district within any school district.

Section 7. Levies for School Purposes

All levies that may be laid by any county or district for the purpose of free schools shall be reported to the clerk of the county court, and shall, under such regulations as may be prescribed by law, be collected by the sheriff, or other collector, who shall make annual settlement with the county court; which settlements shall be made a matter of record by the clerk thereof, in a book to be kept for that purpose.

Section 8.

Repealed

Section 9. Certain Acts Prohibited

No person connected with the free school system of the state, or with any educational institution of any name or grade under state control, shall be interested in the sale, proceeds or profits of any book or other thing used, or to be used therein, under such penalties as may be prescribed by law: Provided, That nothing herein shall be construed to apply to any work written, or thing invented, by such person.

Section 10. Creation of Independent Free School Districts

No independent free school district, or organization shall hereafter be created, except with the consent of the school district or districts out of which the same is to be created, expressed by a majority of the voters voting on the question.

Section 11. Appropriation for State Normal Schools

No appropriation shall hereafter be made to any state normal school, or branch thereof, except to those already established and in operation, or now chartered.

Section 12. Legislature to Foster General School Improvements

The Legislature shall foster and encourage, moral, intellectual, scientific and agricultural improvement; it shall, whenever it may be practicable, make suitable provision for the blind, mute and insane, and for the organization of such institutions of learning as the best interests of general education in the state may demand.

ARTICLE XIII: LAND TITLES

Section 1. Land Titles

All private rights and interests in lands in this state derived from or under the laws of the state of Virginia, and from or under the constitution and laws of this state prior to the time this constitution goes into operation, shall remain valid and secure and shall be determined by the laws in force in Virginia, prior to the formation of this state, and by the constitution and laws in force in this state prior to the time this constitution goes into effect.

Section 2. Land Entry Prohibited

No entry by warrant on land in this state shall hereafter be made.

Section 3.

Repealed

Section 4.

Repealed

Section 5.

Repealed

Section 6.

Repealed

ARTICLE XIV: AMENDMENTS

Section 1. Amendments

No convention shall be called, having the authority to alter the constitution of the state, unless it be in pursuance of law, passed by the affirmative vote of a majority of the members elected to each house of the Legislature and providing that polls shall be opened throughout the state, on the same day therein specified, which shall not be less than three months after the passage of such law, for the purpose of taking the sense of the voters on the question of calling a convention. And such convention shall not be held unless a majority of the votes cast at such polls be in favor of calling the same; nor shall the members be elected to such convention, until, at least, one month after the result of the vote shall be duly ascertained, declared and published. And all acts and ordinances of the said convention shall be submitted to the voters of the State for ratification or rejection, and shall have no validity whatever until they are ratified.

Section 2. How Amendments are Made

Any amendment to the constitution of the state may be proposed in either house of the Legislature at any regular or extraordinary session thereof; and if the same, being read on three several days in each house, be agreed to on its third reading, by two thirds of the members elected thereto, the proposed amendment, with the yeas and nays thereon, shall be entered on the journals, and it shall be the duty of the Legislature to provide by law for submitting the same to the voters of the state for ratification or rejection, at a special election, or at the next general election thereafter, and cause the same to be published, at least three months before such election in some newspaper in every county in which a newspaper is printed. If a majority of the qualified voters, voting on the question at the polls held pursuant to such law, ratify the proposed amendment, it shall be in force from the time of such ratification, as part of the constitution of the state. If two or more amendments be submitted at the same time, the vote on the ratification or rejection shall be taken on each separately, but an amendment may relate to a single subject or to related subject matters and may amend or modify as many articles and as many sections of the constitution as may be necessary and appropriate in order to accomplish the objectives of the amendment. Whenever one or more amendments are submitted at a special election, no other question, issue or matter shall be voted upon at such special election, and the cost of such special election throughout the state shall be paid out of the state treasury.

AMENDMENTS TO THE CONSTITUTION

Amendment 1. THE JUDICIAL AMENDMENT

The supreme court of appeals shall consist of five judges. Those judges in office when this amendment takes effect shall continue in office until their terms shall expire and the Legislature shall provide for the election of an additional judge of said court at the next general election, whose term shall begin on the first day of January, one thousand nine hundred and five, and the governor shall, as for a vacancy, appoint a judge of said court to hold office until the first day of January, one thousand nine hundred and five. The judges of the supreme court of appeals and of the circuit courts shall receive such salaries as shall be fixed by law, for those now in or those hereafter to come into office.

Amendment 2. THE IRREDUCIBLE SCHOOL FUND AMENDMENT

The accumulation of the school fund provided for in section four of article twelve, of the constitution of this state, shall cease upon the adoption of this amendment, and all money to the credit of said fund over one million dollars, together with the interest on said fund, shall be used for the support of free schools of this state.

All money and taxes heretofore payable into the treasury under the provisions of said section four, to the credit of the school fund, shall be hereafter paid into the treasury to the credit of the general school fund for the support of the free schools of the state.

Amendment 3. THE GOOD ROADS AMENDMENT OF 1920

The Legislature shall make provision by law for a system of state roads and highways connecting at least the various county seats of the state, and to be under the control and supervision of such state officers and agencies as may be prescribed by law. The

Legislature shall also provide a state revenue to build, construct, and maintain, or assist in building, constructing and maintaining the same and for that purpose shall have power to authorize the issuing and selling of state bonds, the aggregate outstanding amount of which, at any one time, shall not exceed fifty million dollars.

When a bond issue as aforesaid is authorized, the Legislature shall at the same time provide for the collection of an annual state tax sufficient to pay annually the interest on such debt, and the principal thereof within and not exceeding thirty years.

Amendment 4. THE GOOD ROADS AMENDMENT OF 1928

The Legislature shall have power to authorize the issuing and selling of state bonds not exceeding in the aggregate thirty-five million dollars in addition to the state bonds which were authorized to be issued and sold by the amendment to the constitution proposed by Senate Joint Resolution No. 15, adopted February 15, 1919, and afterwards ratified by a vote of the people. The proceeds of said additional bonds hereby authorized to be issued and sold shall be used and appropriated solely for the building and constructing, or for the assisting in building and constructing the system of state roads and highways provided for by the amendment to the constitution above mentioned.

When a bond issue as aforesaid is authorized, the Legislature shall at the same time provide for the collection of an annual state tax sufficient to pay annually the interest on such debt and to pay the principal thereof within and not exceeding thirty years.

Amendment 5. FIFTY MILLION DOLLAR BOND ISSUE FOR ROADS AMENDMENT

The Legislature shall have power to authorize the issuing and selling of state bonds not exceeding in the aggregate fifty million dollars in addition to the state bonds which were authorized to be issued and sold by the amendment to the constitution proposed by Senate Joint Resolution No. 15, adopted February fifteenth, one thousand nine hundred nineteen, and afterwards ratified by a vote of the people, and Senate Joint Resolution No. 17, adopted by the Legislature at the regular session, one thousand nine hundred twenty-seven, and afterwards ratified by a vote of the people. The proceeds of said additional bonds hereby authorized to be issued and sold shall be used and appropriated solely for the building and construction, or for assisting in building and constructing a system of state secondary roads and highways.

When a bond issue as aforesaid is authorized, the Legislature shall at the same time provide for the collection of an annual state tax sufficient to pay annually the interest on such debt and to pay the principal thereof within and not exceeding thirty years.

Amendment 6. VETERANS BONUS AMENDMENT

The Legislature shall by law provide for the issuance and sale of state bonds, not to exceed in the aggregate ninety million dollars, which shall be in addition to all other state bonds heretofore authorized. The proceeds of such additional bonds, or so many thereof as may be necessary for the purpose, shall be used and appropriated solely for the purpose of paying a cash bonus to veterans of World War I and World War II. Such bonus shall be paid to all persons who rendered active service in the armed forces of the United States in World War I between the sixth day of April, one thousand nine hundred seventeen, and the eleventh day of November, one thousand nine hundred eighteen, both dates inclusive, or in World War II between the seventh day of December, one thousand nine hundred forty-one, and the second day of September, one thousand nine hundred forty-five, both dates inclusive, or in both such wars, who were bona fide residents of the state of West Virginia at the time of their entry into such service and for a period of at least six months prior thereto, who were not dishonorably discharged from such forces, and who within the periods specified above actively served in such armed forces for a period of at least ninety days. Such a bonus shall also be paid to any disabled veteran, otherwise qualified, who was discharged within ninety days after entering the services because of a service-connected disability. The amount of such bonus shall be calculated on the basis of ten dollars for each month, or major fraction thereof, served within the territorial limits of the forty-eight states and the District of Columbia, and fifteen dollars for each month, or major fraction thereof, served outside such limits, but such amount shall in no case exceed three hundred dollars for those who served only within the territorial limits specified above, and four hundred dollars for those who served outside such limits. The bonus to which any deceased veteran would be entitled, if living, shall be paid only to the following surviving relatives of such veteran, if such relatives are residents of this state when application for payment is made: Any unremarried widow, or if none, any child or children under the age of sixteen, or if none, any dependent parent or parents.

Whenever the Legislature shall provide for the issuance of any bonds under the authority of this amendment, it shall at the same time provide for the levy and collection of an additional cigarette tax, or an additional tax on nonintoxicating beer, or an additional charge on the sale of each bottle of wine and liquor, or an additional general consumers sales tax, or a graduated income tax, or any two or more thereof, in such amount as may be required to pay annually the interest on such bonds and the principal thereof within and not exceeding thirty years.

Amendment 7. KOREAN VETERANS BONUS AMENDMENT

The Legislature shall by law provide for the issuance and sale of state bonds which shall be in addition to all other state bonds heretofore issued, for the following purposes:

(1) The paying of a cash bonus to veterans of the armed forces of the United States who served during the Korean conflict. Such bonus shall be paid to all persons who rendered active service in the armed forces of the United States between the twenty-seventh day of June, one thousand nine hundred fifty, and the twenty-seventh day of July, one thousand nine hundred fifty-three, both dates inclusive, who were bona fide residents of the state of West Virginia at the time of their entry into such service and for a period of at least six months prior thereto, who were not dishonorably discharged from such service, and who within the period specified above actively served in such armed forces for a period of at least ninety days. Such a bonus shall also be paid to any disabled veteran, otherwise qualified, who was discharged within ninety days after entering the services because of a service-connected disability. The amount of such bonus shall be calculated on the basis of ten dollars for each month, or major fraction thereof, served within the territorial limits of the forty-eight states and the District of Columbia, and fifteen dollars for each month, or major fraction thereof, served outside such limits, but such amount shall in no case exceed three hundred dollars for those who served only within the territorial limits specified above, and four hundred dollars for those who served outside such limits. The bonus to which any deceased veteran would be entitled, if living, shall be paid only to the following surviving relatives of such veteran, if such relatives are residents of this state when application for payment is made: Any unmarried widow, or if none, any child or children under the age of sixteen, or if none, any dependent parent or parents.

The principal amount of bonds to be issued for the purpose provided in paragraph (1) above shall not exceed the principal amount of the ninety million dollars bonds authorized by the veterans bonus amendment submitted by chapter nineteen of the acts of the Legislature of West Virginia of one thousand nine hundred forty-nine, regular session, and ratified by the people of West Virginia at the general election held on the seventh day of November, one thousand nine hundred fifty (hereinafter referred to as "Veterans Bonus Amendment of One Thousand Nine Hundred Fifty"), which shall not have been issued on the date of the ratification of this amendment by the people of West Virginia: Provided, however, That such bonds issued under the provisions of paragraph (1) above may be funded or refunded at any time in the manner provided in paragraph (2) below.

(2) The funding or refunding of all or any part of the bonds heretofore issued pursuant to said veterans bonus amendment of one thousand nine hundred fifty. Said bonds issued pursuant to said veterans bonus amendment of one thousand nine hundred fifty may be so funded or refunded either on the maturity dates of said bonds or on any date on which said bonds are callable prior to maturity, and if any of said bonds have not matured or are not then callable prior to maturity, the Legislature may nevertheless provide at any time for the issuance of refunding bonds to fund or refund such bonds on the dates when said bonds mature or on any date on which said bonds are callable prior to maturity, and for the investment or reinvestment of the proceeds of such refunding bonds in direct obligations of the United States of America until the date or dates upon which such bonds issued pursuant to said veterans bonus amendment of one thousand nine hundred fifty mature or are callable prior to maturity.

The principal amount of bonds issued under the provisions of paragraph (2) above shall not exceed the principal amount of the bonds to be funded or refunded thereby.

Such bonds for the purposes authorized in paragraphs (1) and (2) above may be issued from time to time as separate issues for such purposes or as combined issues for such purposes.

Whenever the Legislature shall provide for the issuance of any bonds under the authority of this amendment, it shall at the same time provide for the levy and collection of an additional cigarette tax, or an additional tax on nonintoxicating beer, or an additional charge on the sale of each bottle of wine and liquor, or an additional general consumers sales tax, or a graduated income tax, or any two or more thereof, in such amount as may be required to pay annually the interest on such bonds and the principal thereof within and not exceeding thirty years, and all such taxes or charges so levied shall be irrevocably dedicated for the payment of the principal of and interest on such bonds until such principal of and interest on such bonds is finally paid and discharged, and any of the covenants, agreements or provisions in the acts of the Legislature levying such taxes or charges shall be enforceable in any court of competent jurisdiction by any of the holders of said bonds. The additional taxes on cigarettes and nonintoxicating beer and additional charges on the sale of each bottle of alcoholic liquor provided for in chapters six, one hundred eighty-four and one hundred eighty-seven of the acts of the Legislature of West Virginia, regular session, one thousand nine hundred fifty-one, shall continue to be pledged for the payment of the principal of and interest on bonds issued pursuant to said veterans bonus amendment of one thousand nine hundred fifty, or bonds issued pursuant to this amendment to fund or refund such bonds issued pursuant to said veterans bonus amendment of one thousand nine hundred fifty: Provided, however, That upon the funding or refunding of all outstanding bonds issued pursuant to said veterans bonus amendment of one thousand nine hundred fifty, or the deposit in trust of sufficient funds to pay all the principal of and interest on such outstanding bonds issued pursuant to said veterans bonus amendment of one thousand nine hundred fifty to their respective dates of maturity or to the first date upon which said bonds are callable prior to maturity, the taxes and charges provided for in said chapters six, one hundred eighty- four and one hundred eighty-seven of the acts of the Legislature of West Virginia, regular session, one thousand nine hundred fifty-one, may be pledged to the payment of the principal of and interest on any bonds issued under any of the provisions of this amendment.

Amendment 8. BETTER ROADS AMENDMENT

The Legislature shall have power to authorize the issuing and selling of state bonds not exceeding in the aggregate two hundred million dollars. The proceeds of said bonds hereby authorized to be issued and sold shall be used and appropriated solely for the building and construction of state roads and highways provided for by this constitution and the laws enacted thereunder. Such bonds may be issued and sold in amounts not to exceed twenty million dollars in any fiscal year. When a bond issue as aforesaid is authorized, the Legislature shall, at the same time provide for the collection of an annual state tax sufficient to pay as it may accrue the interest on such bonds and the principal thereof within and not exceeding twenty-five years. Such tax shall be levied in any year only to the extent that the moneys in the state road fund irrevocably set aside and appropriated for and applied to the payment of the interest on and principal of said bonds becoming due and payable in such year are insufficient therefor.

The authority to issue and sell and have outstanding additional bonds granted by the amendment to the constitution proposed by Senate Joint Resolution No. 15, adopted February 15, 1919, and afterwards ratified by a vote of the people, is hereby revoked as of January 1, 1965, but said amendment shall in all other respects remain in full force and effect.

Amendment 9. ROADS DEVELOPMENT AMENDMENT

The Legislature shall have power to authorize the issuing and selling of state bonds not exceeding in the aggregate three hundred fifty million dollars. The proceeds of said bonds hereby authorized to be issued and sold shall be used and appropriated solely for the building and construction of free state roads and highways provided for by this constitution and the laws enacted thereunder. When a bond issue as aforesaid is authorized, the Legislature shall, at the same time provide for the collection of an annual state tax sufficient to pay as it may accrue the interest on such bonds and the principal thereof within and not exceeding twenty-five years. Such tax shall be levied in any year only to the extent that the moneys in the state road fund irrevocably set aside and appropriated for and applied to the payment of the interest on and principal of said bonds becoming due and payable in such year are insufficient therefor.

Amendment 10. BETTER SCHOOL BUILDINGS AMENDMENT

The Legislature shall have power to authorize the issuing and selling of state bonds, not exceeding in the aggregate two hundred million dollars, which shall be in addition to all other state bonds heretofore authorized. The proceeds of the bonds hereby authorized to be issued and sold shall, notwithstanding the provisions of section six, article ten of this constitution or any other provision of this constitution to the contrary, be distributed to such county boards of education as qualify therefor by meeting such conditions, qualifications and requirements as shall be prescribed by general law and used and appropriated by such county boards of education solely for the construction, renovation or remodeling of elementary or secondary public school buildings or facilities, the equipping of the same in connection with any such construction, renovation or remodeling and the acquisition and preparation of sites for elementary or secondary public school buildings or facilities. Such bonds may be issued and sold at such time or times and in such amount or amounts as the Legislature shall authorize. When a bond issue as aforesaid is authorized, the Legislature shall at the same time provide for the collection of an annual state tax sufficient to pay as it may accrue the interest on such bonds and the principal thereof within and not exceeding thirty-four years, and all such taxes so levied shall be irrevocably dedicated for the payment of principal of and interest on such bonds until such principal of and interest on such bonds are finally paid and discharged, and any of the covenants, agreements or provisions in the acts of the legislature levying such taxes shall be enforceable in any court of competent jurisdiction by any of the holders of the bonds.

Amendment 11. BETTER HIGHWAYS AMENDMENT

The Legislature shall have power to authorize the issuing and selling of state bonds not exceeding in the aggregate five hundred million dollars. The proceeds of said bonds hereby authorized to be issued and sold shall be used and appropriated solely for the following purposes and in the following amounts:

(1) One hundred twenty million dollars for bridge replacement and improvement program;

(2) One hundred thirty million dollars for completion of the Appalachian highway system;

(3) Fifty million dollars for upgrading sections of trunkline and feeder systems;

(4) Fifty million dollars for upgrading West Virginia State Route 2;

(5) One hundred million dollars for upgrading state and local service roads;

(6) Fifty million dollars for construction, reconstruction, improving and upgrading of U.S. Route 52 between Huntington and Bluefield, West Virginia.

When a bond issue as aforesaid is authorized, the Legislature shall at the same time provide for the collection of an annual state tax sufficient to pay as it may accrue the interest on such bonds and the principal thereof within and not exceeding twenty-five years. Such tax shall be levied in any year only to the extent that the moneys in the state road fund irrevocably set aside and appropriated for and applied to the payment of the interest on and the principal of said bonds becoming due and payable in such year are insufficient therefor.

Amendment 12. VIETNAM VETERANS BONUS AMENDMENT

The Legislature shall provide by law, either for the appropriation from the general revenues of the state, or for the issuance and sale of state bonds, which shall be in addition to all other state bonds heretofore issued, or a combination of both as the Legislature may determine, for the purpose of paying a cash bonus to veterans of the armed forces of the United States who were in active service during the periods hereinafter described.

Such bonus shall be paid to all persons who rendered active service in the armed forces of the United States between the first day of August, one thousand nine hundred sixty-four, and the date determined by the president or Congress of the United States as the end of involvement of United States armed forces in the Vietnam conflict, both dates inclusive, who were bona fide residents of the state of West Virginia at the time of their entry into such active service and for a period of at least six months immediately prior thereto, who have not been separated from such service under conditions other than honorable, and who, within the period specified above, actively served in such armed forces for a period of at least ninety days. Such bonus shall also be paid to any person, otherwise eligible under the preceding sentence, who rendered active service in the armed forces of the United States prior to the first day of August, one thousand nine hundred sixty-four, and who received the Vietnam armed forces expeditionary medal. Such bonus shall also be paid to any veteran, otherwise qualified under either of the two sentences next preceding, who was discharged within ninety days after entering the armed forces because of a service-connected disability. The amount of such bonus shall be calculated on the basis of twenty dollars per month for each month of active service, or major fraction thereof, for veterans who received the Vietnam armed forces expeditionary medal or the Vietnam service medal, up to four hundred dollars, and ten dollars per month for each month of active service, or major fraction thereof, for veterans who have not received the Vietnam armed forces expeditionary medal or the Vietnam service medal, up to three hundred dollars. Not more than one bonus shall be paid to or on behalf of the service of any one veteran.

The bonus to which any deceased veteran would have been entitled, if living, shall be paid to the following surviving relatives of such veteran, if such relatives are residents of the state when such application is made and if such relatives are living at the time payment is made: Any unremarried widow or widower, or, if none, all children, stepchildren and adopted children under the age of eighteen, or, if none, any parent, stepparent, adoptive parent or person standing in loco parentis. The categories of persons listed shall be treated as separate categories listed in order of entitlement and where there be more than one member of a class, the bonus shall be paid to each member according to his proportional share. Where a deceased veteran's death was connected with such service and resulted from such service during the time period specified, however, the surviving relatives shall be paid, in accordance with the same order of entitlement, the sum of five hundred dollars in lieu of any bonus to which the deceased might have been entitled if living.

The principal amount of any bonds issued for the purpose of paying the bonuses provided for in this amendment shall not exceed the principal amount of forty million dollars, but may be funded or refunded either on the maturity dates of said bonds or on any date on which said bonds are callable prior to maturity, and if any of said bonds have not matured or are not then callable prior to maturity, the Legislature may nevertheless provide at any time for the issuance of refunding bonds to fund or refund such bonds on the dates when said bonds mature or on any date on which said bonds are callable prior to maturity and for the investment or reinvestment of the proceeds of such refunding bonds in direct obligations of the United States of America until the date or dates upon which such bonds mature or are callable prior to maturity. The principal amount of any refunding bonds issued under the provisions of this paragraph shall not exceed the principal amount of the bonds to be funded or refunded thereby.

The bonds may be issued from time to time for the purposes authorized by this amendment as separate issues or as combined issues.

Whenever the Legislature shall provide for the issuance of any bonds under the authority of this amendment, it shall at the same time provide for the levy and collection of an additional cigarette tax, or a tax on any other tobacco products, or an additional tax on nonintoxicating beer, or an additional charge on the sale of each bottle of wine and liquor, or an additional general consumers sales tax, or a graduated income tax, or any combination of one or more thereof, or such other dedicated tax as the Legislature may determine, in such amount as may be required to pay annually the interest on such bonds and the principal thereof within and not exceeding thirty years, and all such taxes or charges so levied shall be irrevocably dedicated for the payment of the principal of and interest on such bonds until such principal of and interest on such bonds are finally paid and discharged and any of the covenants, agreements or provisions in the acts of the Legislature levying such taxes or charges shall be enforceable in any court of competent jurisdiction by any of the holders of said bonds.

The Legislature shall have the power to enact legislation necessary and proper to implement the provisions of this amendment.

Amendment 13. QUALIFIED VETERANS HOUSING BONDS AMENDMENT.

I. The Legislature shall have the power to authorize the issuing and selling of general obligation bonds of the State which shall be in addition to all other state bonds heretofore authorized. The aggregate annual amount payable on all such bonds, including both principal and interest, shall be limited such that the debt service accruing on such bonds in any fiscal year shall not exceed $35,000,000, exclusive of any amounts payable on such bonds for which moneys or securities have been irrevocably set aside and dedicated solely for the purpose of such payment. The proceeds of the bonds hereby authorized to be issued and sold shall be used and appropriated to provide financing for owner-occupied residences for persons determined by the Legislature to be qualified veterans, except that:

(i) Part of the proceeds from each separate issuance of bonds may be set aside as a reserve for the purposes of the Veterans' Mortgage Fund herein authorized; and

(ii) proceeds may be dedicated for the payment of principal, redemption price or interest on any such bonds to be refunded. Such bonds may be issued and sold at such time or times and in such amount or amounts as the Legislature shall authorize. All proceeds of such bonds, and all revenues derived from the use and investment of such proceeds, shall be deposited in a separate fund of the State, designated as the Veterans' Mortgage Fund. Amounts in such fund shall be used solely for the purposes of making loans for qualified veterans, providing for the payment or redemption of such bonds and the interest thereon, and providing for the payment of necessary expenses in connection therewith. When a bond issue as aforesaid is authorized, the Legislature shall at the same time provide for the collection of an annual state tax sufficient to pay as it may accrue the interest on such bonds and the principal thereof within and not exceeding forty years, and all such taxes so levied shall be irrevocably dedicated for the payment of principal of and interest on such bonds until the obligation of the State with respect to the payment of such principal and interest has been discharged, and any of the covenants, agreements or provisions in the Acts of the Legislature levying such taxes shall be enforceable in any court of competent jurisdiction by any of the holders of such bonds. Such tax shall be levied in any year only to the extent that the moneys on deposit in the Veteran's Mortgage Fund are insufficient to pay all amounts accruing on such bonds in such year.

II. The Legislature shall have the power to enact legislation to implement the provisions of this amendment.

Amendment 14. VETERANS BONUS AMENDMENT

(Persian Gulf, Lebanon, Grenada and Panama)

The Legislature shall provide by law, either for the appropriation from the general revenues of the State, or for the issuance and sale of state bonds, which shall be in addition to all other state bonds heretofore issued, or a combination of both as the Legislature may determine, for the purpose of paying a cash bonus to veterans of the armed forces of the United States who

(1) served on active duty, or who were members of reserve components called to active duty by the President of the United States under Title 10, United States Code section 782(D), 783, or 783(B), during the Persian Gulf conflict, Operation Desert Shield/Desert Storm, between the first day of August, one thousand nine hundred ninety and the date determined by the president or congress of the United States as the end of the involvement of the United States armed forces in the Persian Gulf conflict, both dates inclusive; or

(2) veterans, active service members, or members of reserve components, of the armed forces of the United States, who served on active duty in one of the military operations for which he or she received a campaign badge or expeditionary medal during the periods hereinafter described. For purposes of this amendment, periods of active duty in a campaign or expedition are designated as: The conflict in Panama, between the twentieth day of December, one thousand nine hundred eighty-nine, through the thirty-first day of January, one thousand nine hundred ninety, both dates inclusive; the conflict in Grenada, between the twenty-third day of October, one thousand nine hundred eighty-three, and the twenty-first day of November, one thousand nine hundred eighty-three, both dates inclusive; and the conflict in Lebanon, between the twenty-fifth day of August, one thousand nine hundred eighty-two, and the twenty-sixth day of February, one thousand nine hundred eighty-four, both dates inclusive. For purposes of this amendment not more than one bonus shall be paid to or on behalf of the service of any one veteran. In order to be eligible to receive a bonus, such persons must have been bona fide residents of the State of West Virginia at the time of their entry into such active service and for a period of at least six months immediately prior thereto, who have not been separated from such service under conditions other than honorable. Such bonus shall also be paid to any veteran,

otherwise qualified under the two sentences next preceding, who was discharged within ninety days after entering the armed forces because of a service-connected disability. The amount of such bonus shall be five hundred dollars per eligible person who was in active service, inside the combat zone designated by the President or Congress of the United States at anytime during the dates specified hereinabove. In the case of the Persian Gulf conflict, the amount of bonus shall be three hundred dollars per eligible person who was in active service outside of the combat zone designated by the President or Congress of the United States during the dates specified hereinabove. The bonus to which any deceased veteran would have been entitled, if living, shall be paid to the following surviving relatives of such veterans, if such relatives are residents of the State when such application is made and if such relatives are living at the time payment is made: Any unremarried widow or widower, or, if none, all children, stepchildren and adopted children under the age of eighteen, or, if none, any parent, stepparent, adoptive parent or person standing in loco parentis. The categories of persons listed shall be treated as separate categories listed in order of entitlement and where there be more than one member of a class, the bonus shall be paid to each member according to his proportional share. Where a deceased veteran's death was connected with such service and resulted from such service during the time period specified, however, the surviving relatives shall be paid, in acccrdance with the same order of entitlement, the sum of one thousand dollars in lieu of any bonus to which the deceased might have been entitled if living.

The principal amount of any bonds issued for the purpose of paying the bonuses provided for in this amendment shall not exceed the principal amount of four million dollars, but may be funded or refunded either on the maturity dates of said bonds or on any date on which said bonds are callable prior to maturity, and if any of said bonds have not matured or are not then callable prior to maturity, the Legislature may nevertheless provide at any time for the issuance of refunding bonds to fund or refund such bonds on the dates when said bonds mature or on any date on which said bonds are callable prior to maturity and for the investment or reinvestment of the proceeds of such refunding bonds in direct obligations of the United States of America until the date or dates upon which such bonds mature or are callable prior to maturity. The principal amount of any refunding bonds issued under the provisions of this paragraph shall not exceed the principal amount of the bonds to be funded or refunded thereby.

The bonds may be issued from time to time for the purposes authorized by this amendment as separate issues or as combined issues.

Whenever the Legislature shall provide for the issuance of any bonds under the authority of this amendment, it shall at the same time provide for the levy, collection and dedication of an additional tax, or enhancement to such other tax as the Legislature may determine, in such amount as may be required to pay annually the interest on such bonds and the principal thereof within and not exceeding fifteen years, and all such taxes or charges so levied shall be irrevocably dedicated for the payment of the principal of and interest on such bonds until such principal of and interest on such bonds are finally paid and discharged and any of the covenants, agreements or provisions in the acts of the Legislature levying such taxes or charges shall be enforceable in any court of competent jurisdiction by any of the holders of said bonds. Any revenue generated in excess of that which is required to pay the bonuses provided herein and to pay any administrative cost associated with such payment shall be used to pay the principal and interest on any bonds issued as soon as is economically practicable.

The Legislature shall have the power to enact legislation necessary and proper to implement the provisions of this amendment.

Amendment 15. INFRASTRUCTURE IMPROVEMENT AMENDMENT

I. The Legislature shall have power to authorize the issuing and selling of state bonds not exceeding in the aggregate three hundred million dollars, which shall be in addition to all other bonds heretofore authorized. The proceeds of said bonds hereby authorized to be issued and sold shall be used and appropriated solely for the construction, extension, expansion, rehabilitation, repair and improvement of water supply and sewage treatment systems and for the acquisition, preparation, construction and improvement of sites for economic development in this state in a manner and subject to such conditions, qualifications and requirements as shall be prescribed by general law. Such bonds may be issued and sold at such time or times and in such amount or amounts as the Legislature shall authorize. When a bond issue as aforesaid is authorized, the Legislature shall, at the same time, provide for the irrevocable dedication, prior to the application of such tax proceeds for any other purpose, of an annual portion of any gross receipts tax which is then currently imposed on businesses that sever, extract and, or produce natural resources within this state which will be suficient to pay, as it may accrue, the interest on such bonds and the principal thereof, within and not exceeding thirty years and all such taxes so levied and the additional tax hereinafter described shall be irrevocably dedicated to such purpose until such principal and interest on such bonds are finally paid and discharged: Provided, That when a bond issue as aforesaid is authorized, the Legislature shall at the same time provide for the collection of an additional annual state tax sufficient to pay as it may accrue the interest on such bonds and the principal thereof within and not exceeding thirty years: Provided, however, That such additional tax shall be levied in any year only to the extent that the moneys from the tax previously dedicated herein are insufficient therefor. Any of the covenants, agreements or provisions in the acts of the Legislature levying and dedicating such taxes shall be enforceable in any court of competent jurisdiction by any of the holders of the bonds.

II. The Legislature shall have power to enact legislation to implement the provisions of this amendment.

Amendment 16. SAFE ROADS AMENDMENT OF 1996

(a) The Legislature shall have power to authorize the issuing and selling of state bonds not exceeding in the aggregate five hundred fifty million dollars. The proceeds of said bonds hereby authorized to be issued and sold over a five-year period in the following amounts:

(1) The first day of July, one thousand nine hundred ninety-seven, one hundred ten million dollars;

(2) The first day of July, one thousand nine hundred ninety-eight, one hundred ten million dollars;

(3) The first day of July, one thousand nine hundred ninety-nine, one hundred ten million dollars;

(4) The first day of July, two thousand, one hundred ten million dollars;

(5) The first day of July, two thousand one, one hundred ten million dollars.

Any bonds not issued under the provisions of subdivisions (1) through (4) of this subsection may be carried forward and issued in any subsequent year.

(b) The proceeds of the bonds shall be used and appropriated for the following purposes:

(1) Matching available federal funds for highway construction in this state; and

(2) General highway construction or improvements in each of the fifty-five counties.

(c) When a bond issue as aforesaid is authorized, the Legislature shall at the same time provide for the collection of an annual state tax sufficient to pay as it may accrue the interest on such bonds and the principal thereof within and not exceeding twenty-five years. Such tax shall be levied in any year only to the extent that the moneys in the state road fund irrevocably set aside and appropriated for and applied to the payment of the interest on and the principal of said bonds becoming due and payable in such year are insufficient therefor. Any interest that accrues on the issued bonds prior to payment shall only be used for the purposes of the bonds.

Amendment 17. VETERANS BONUS AMENDMENT

(Kosovo, Afghanistan, and Iraq)

The Legislature shall provide by law, either for the appropriation from the general revenues of the State, or for the issuance and sale of state bonds, which shall be in addition to all other state bonds heretofore issued, or a combination of both as the Legislature may determine, for the purpose of paying a cash bonus to:

(1) Veterans of the armed forces of the United States who served on active duty in areas of conflict in Iraq, or were members of reserve components called to active duty by the President of the United States under Title 10, United States Code section 12301, 12302, 12303 or 12304 during the Iraqi War, between the nineteenth day of March, two thousand three and the date determined by the President or Congress of the United States as the end of the involvement of the United States armed forces in Iraq, both dates inclusive; or

(2) veterans, active service members, or members of reserve components of the armed forces of the United States, who served on active duty in one of the military operations for which he or she received a campaign badge or expeditionary medal during the periods hereinafter described. For purposes of this amendment, periods of active duty in a campaign or expedition are designated as: The conflict in Kosovo between the twentieth day of November, one thousand nine hundred ninety-five and the thirty-first day of December, two thousand, both dates inclusive; and the conflict in Afghanistan, between the seventh day of October, two thousand one and the date determined by the President or Congress of the United States as the end of the involvement of the United States armed forces in Afghanistan, both dates inclusive. For purposes of this amendment not more than one bonus shall be paid to or on behalf of the service of a veteran. In order to be eligible to receive a bonus, a veteran must have been a bona fide resident of the State of West Virginia at the time of his or her entry into active service and for a period of at least six months immediately prior thereto, and has not been separated from service under conditions other than honorable. The bonus shall also be paid to any veteran otherwise qualified pursuant to this amendment, who was discharged within ninety days after entering the armed forces because of a service-connected disability. The amount of the bonus shall be six hundred dollars per eligible veteran who was in active service, inside the combat zone in Kosovo, Afghanistan or Iraq as designated by the President or Congress of the United States at anytime during the dates specified hereinabove. In the case of the Iraqi War and the conflict in Afghanistan, the amount of bonus shall be four hundred dollars per eligible veteran who was in active service outside the combat zone designated by the President or Congress of the United States during the dates specified hereinabove. The bonus to which any deceased veteran would have been entitled, if living, shall be paid to the following surviving relatives of the veteran, if the relatives are residents of the State when the application is made and if the relatives are living at the time payment is made: Any unremarried widow or widower, or, if none, all children, stepchildren and adopted children under the age of eighteen, or, if none, any parent, stepparent, adoptive parent or person standing in loco parentis. The categories of persons listed shall be treated as separate categories listed in order of entitlement and where there is more than one member of a class, the bonus shall be paid to each member according to his or her proportional share. Where a deceased veteran?s death was connected with the service and resulted from the service during the time period specified, however, the surviving relatives shall be paid, in accordance with the same order of entitlement, the sum of two thousand dollars in lieu of any bonus to which the deceased might have been entitled if living. The person receiving the bonus shall not be required to include the bonus as income for state income tax purposes.

The principal amount of any bonds issued for the purpose of paying the bonuses provided for in this amendment shall not exceed the principal amount of eight million dollars, but may be funded or refunded either on the maturity dates of the bonds or on any date on which the bonds are callable prior to maturity, and if any of the bonds have not matured or are not then callable prior to maturity, the Legislature may nevertheless provide at any time for the issuance of refunding bonds to fund or refund the bonds on the dates when the bonds mature or on any date on which the bonds are callable prior to maturity and for the investment or reinvestment of the proceeds of the refunding bonds in direct obligations of the United States of America until the date or dates upon which the bonds mature or are callable prior to maturity. The principal amount of any refunding bonds issued under the provisions of this paragraph shall not exceed the principal amount of the bonds to be funded or refunded thereby.

The bonds may be issued from time to time for the purposes authorized by this amendment as separate issues or as combined issues.

Whenever the Legislature shall provide for the issuance of any bonds under the authority of this amendment, it shall at the same time provide for the levy, collection and dedication of an additional tax, or enhancement to another tax as the Legislature may determine, in an amount as may be required to pay annually the interest on the bonds and the principal thereof within and not exceeding fifteen years, and all taxes or charges so levied shall be irrevocably dedicated for the payment of the principal of and interest on the bonds until the principal of and interest on the bonds are finally paid and discharged and any of the covenants, agreements or provisions in the acts of the Legislature levying the taxes or charges shall be enforceable in any court of competent jurisdiction by any of the holders of said bonds. Any revenue generated in excess of that which is required to pay the bonuses herein and to pay any administrative cost associated with the payment shall be used to pay the principal and interest on any bonds issued as soon as is economically practicable.

The Legislature shall have the power to enact legislation necessary and proper to implement the provisions of this amendment: Provided, That no bonus may be issued until the Governor certifies a list of veterans and relatives of deceased veterans eligible to receive such bonus to the Legislature at any regular or special session of the Legislature as the Legislature will provide by general law.

Amendment 18. Roads to Prosperity Amendment of 2017

(a) The Legislature shall have power to authorize the issuing and selling of state bonds not exceeding in the aggregate $1.6 billion. The proceeds of said bonds are hereby authorized to be issued and sold over a four-year period in the following amounts:

(1) July 1, 2017, an amount not to exceed $800 million;

(2) July 1, 2018, an amount not to exceed $400 million;

(3) July 1, 2019, an amount not to exceed $200 million; and

(4) July 1, 2020, an amount not to exceed $200 million

Any bonds not issued under the provisions of subdivisions (1) through (3), inclusive, of this subsection may be carried forward and issued in any subsequent year before July 1, 2021.

(b) The proceeds of the bonds shall be used and appropriated for the following purposes:

(1) Matching available federal funds for highway and bridge construction in this state; and

(2) General highway and secondary road and bridge construction or improvements in each of the fifty-five counties.

(c) When a bond issue as aforesaid is authorized, the Legislature shall at the same time provide for the collection of an annual state tax which shall be in a sufficient amount to pay the interest on such bonds and the principal thereof as such may accrue within and not exceeding twenty-five years. Such taxes shall be levied in any year only to the extent that the moneys in the state road fund irrevocably set aside and appropriated for and applied to the payment of the interest on and the principal of said bonds becoming due and payable in such year are insufficient therefor. Any interest that accrues on the issued bonds prior to payment shall only be used for the purposes of the bonds.

www.ingramcontent.com/pod-product-compliance
Lightning Source LLC
Chambersburg PA
CBHW071553220526
45469CB00003B/1007